QML UNLOCKED

From Curiosity to Capability in Quantum Machine Learning

JAVIER MANCILLA MONTERO

QML UNLOCKED

From Curiosity to Capability in Quantum machine Learning

Copyright © 2025 by Javier Mancilla Montero

Interior design by Saqib

First Printing 2025

Printed in the United States of America

DEDICATION

To all my brilliant colleagues who spend their days (and way too many late nights) wrestling with different quantum techniques, algorithms, and the dream of making quantum machine learning more useful and in a broader market sense.

And, of course, to my wonderful wife, Sandy, and our three incredible kids, Agustín, Francisco, and Máximo—who remind me daily that, no matter how complex quantum mechanics gets, nothing is more rewarding than family life. You are the true force that keeps my universe in balance.

ACKNOWLEDGEMENTS

Writing this book has been an intense and rewarding journey, but I certainly didn't take it alone. I am deeply grateful to those who helped shape and refine these ideas, ensuring that the content is both rigorous and practical.

First, my sincere thanks to Tomás Tagliani, an exceptional data scientist with a strong foundation in business administration, risk assessment, and financial modeling. His experience at companies like Mercado Libre, HSBC, and Visa, plus his impressive background, allowed him to provide invaluable insights, making sure this book was grounded in real-world applications rather than just theoretical concepts. Tomás approached his role as an editor with the perfect balance of scrutiny and constructive feedback, often catching things I had overlooked and asking the right questions—sometimes the uncomfortable ones that truly needed to be addressed. His ability to view this work from the perspective of the audience made his input indispensable. Tomás, I truly appreciate the effort, patience, and expertise you brought to this project.

I am also profoundly grateful to Theodore Bouloumis, whose background as a PhD in Applied Physics and Nanophotonics, along with his experience in quantum machine learning applied to finance, made him an excellent peer reviewer. His sharp analytical skills and attention to detail ensured that both the chapters and the accompanying code were not only technically sound but also aligned with the broader goals of practical implementation. Theodore has an ability to challenge ideas in a way that strengthens them, making sure that every argument and explanation stands up to rigorous evaluation. His contributions were not just about fixing mistakes but about making the entire work more coherent and insightful.

To both of you, thank you for your patience, your feedback, and for making sure this book wasn't just another collection of abstract ideas but something that could be genuinely useful to those looking to explore quantum machine learning in practice.

FOREWORD

by Tomás Tagliani, Senior Data Scientist and MBA.

If you are reading these lines, this is probably your first interaction with quantum computing. Perhaps you've heard about it before, especially if you've watched NatGeo documentaries about space, like those featuring Carl Sagan or Neil Degrasse Tyson. Or perhaps you learned about it from Sheldon and Leonard while laughing along with an episode from The Big Bang Theory (if you haven't, I strongly recommend it). If that's the case, you probably know about Schrodinger and the cat, Heisenberg and the lost driver, or Einstein and his famous phrase, "God doesn't place dice with the universe". Although these might be easy to understand and even perhaps funny, they are quite far from the actual workings of quantum physics. But don't worry, this book is not about that either.

QML Unlocked is about the specific uses and implementations of quantum computing in the field of machine learning. Although its principles are based on the same ones that backed the Manhattan Project, its applications are quite different. Throughout the following chapters, you will learn about some of these principles, always explained in fairly simple terms and going over the key concepts that impact its uses and fundamentals. And, of course, focusing on its practical applications, where it can be useful and, more importantly, a game changer for some industries.

I've been working with data for the last 10 years. My job title has changed throughout that journey, starting off as a Data

Analyst, then moving to Data Scientist, switching to Machine Learning Engineer when everything became about scalability and GPUs and, more recently, converting to AI Specialist when we started calling everything AI-based. I definitely think my title is going to change again to something involving "quantum" in its title. And this book is an excellent starting point for that. It basically takes the machine learning models we all know very well and explains how, combining them with quantum computing and hardware, we can take them to a whole new level.

When developing models, we know that there are some challenges we just cannot break. So we have found ways around that, working solutions and patches. Quantum computing could (and definitely will) change that paradigm. So, like those who spoke about AI before ChatGPT was released, it's definitely recommendable to get ahead. *QML Unlocked* is your first step down that journey.

Javier Mancilla is an excellent professional, top-notch consultant, both in AI and any project to be honest, one of those people that get stuff done, and that makes other people do stuff. He's one of the best colleagues I've known in my professional career and, more importantly, a personal friend. We've worked together for the last five years, across multiple projects, and he never let me down. Not once. He's always surpassing expectations and textbook overachiever. And he's definitely done it again with this book. It's an excellently written piece of work, where you will find everything you need to know about quantum computing, so you can then dig deeper into whatever resonates with you.

And the cherry on top: code. My strong suggestion is to open this book on one hand and also the code whatever IDE you use on the screen (VS Code is my suggestion if you haven't used one so far). Clone his repo (or copy the code, if that's easier) and follow the chapters doing it by yourself. You'll learn so much. I have, and that's after working side-by-side with Javier in QML for two years now (I'm no expert in Quantum, but this is definitely a bootstrapper in my journey to becoming one).

Although the book is pretty self-explanatory, to get the most out of it, I recommend you follow Javier's instructions carefully. This will help you understand the whole picture while also avoiding getting lost with the terminology, especially through the hardware chapters. Of course, you can always "google" more stuff, but information out there might confuse you even more. Try to match the concepts to stuff you already know, and visualize the effects on the excellent examples Javier has laid out for you. If you do so, I can guarantee you will enjoy this book as much as I did.

If you have diligently followed through and completed your homework, you will be equipped to initiate your own quantum computing project. You will have the necessary tools to understand which technique and hardware better fits your needs. That doesn't mean you won't face obstacles down the road. You will need to fix bugs, solve problems, and work around incompatibilities. But the result will be worth your time. Trust me when I say this will mark a new chapter in your data career. And if you don't have a data career but you want to understand how to use this technology in your company, in your personal life, or if you are just curious, this book is also for you. After completing it, you will understand quantum technology so much better, and you'll be able to read news about it, do deeper research, and swim through the enormous amount of information around this topic.

To sum up, if by the end of chapter 10 you still don't know what quantum means, where to use it, and how you can continue your research, please contact me, and I'll gently explain what you did wrong. Just kidding, but this book is a must-read for anyone starting their quantum machine learning journey, regardless of their background, interests, or future endeavors. To paraphrase Sheldon, in the ever-changing space-time continuum of quantum machine learning, this book would be (0,0,0,0). This is the beginning of an exciting new area of research in your file. Don't miss it!

PREFACE (AND INSTRUCTIONS)

I'm glad to have you here, ready to explore the world of Quantum Machine Learning (QML). Before we begin, let's set the right expectations. If you're an expert in quantum physics, have experience designing quantum circuits, or already work with quantum computing daily, this book might not offer much new for you—though you may find some interesting discussions starting from Chapter 7 onward. However, if you're unfamiliar with QML or have a basic understanding of its concepts, this book is an excellent resource for you.

The goal of this book is to guide you from little or no prior knowledge in QML to a point where you can run your own Python code in Jupyter Notebooks, experiment with real datasets, and understand how these techniques can be applied in practice—whether for a business project, research, or personal curiosity.

A few notes before we get started:

1. No rush into coding. The first half of the book is focused on explanations, so you won't be thrown into technical details right away.

2. No complex formulas. If you're someone who sees an equation and immediately loses interest, don't worry—this book focuses on concepts and intuition rather than mathematical derivations.

3. There's no need to retype everything. When we do get to coding, you don't have to manually write out

every line. A GitHub repository with all the examples is available here: https://github.com/maximer-v/qml-unlocked.

4. Additional resources are available. The repository also includes links to figures, references, and suggestions for further reading.

5. Can you skip straight to the code? That depends on your background. If you already have experience with machine learning and programming, you might choose to dive right into the practical sections. However, if you're newer to the topic, I'd recommend starting from the beginning to build a solid understanding.

With that, let's begin. I hope you find this journey both insightful and rewarding.

TABLE OF CONTENTS

CHAPTER 1

Quantum Computing and Machine Learning

Introduction

Quantum computing is often regarded as the next big step in processing capability. While this is still to become true in the future, quantum computing is getting closer and closer to solve problems that could be considered unreachable for even the most advanced supercomputers. Astonishing, isn't it? And still, you are probably wondering: Why is this important to me, in my projects, my employment, or even my daily life? How can quantum computing change paradigms or affect me in any way?

Throughout this chapter, we'll demystify quantum computing and investigate its intersection with machine learning—a discipline that has already transformed many sectors. We'll examine the principles of quantum computers together, more especially why they are so significant in the context of the data-driven world we live in now.

The fundamental operations behind quantum algorithms entail events that would seem, at first glance, somewhat contradictory or difficult to understand. Concepts such as superposition and entanglement appear akin to science fiction; and the mathematics, going from linear algebra and beyond, can occasionally feel like a foreign language. Nevertheless, don't worry! This book serves as your guide through these complexities. My goal is to give simple and friendly explanations, which provide you access to, and even allow you to enjoy, these difficult ideas.

Foundational ideas

Every computing system is built on top of its basic information unit. In the classical computing paradigm, this unit is the bit. Represented as 0 or 1, a bit is simple, straightforward, and binary. As such, it can exist in either one of two states. From operating a spreadsheet to creating high-definition video, these states are the building blocks for all the amazing things classical computers can do. Imagine building a skyscraper using these blocks, one by one. Just like that, classical computers use each piece of information sequentially to build the final result, starting from clearly defined points.

Now the laws of the game change with the arrival of the qubit (or quantum bit), the quantum counterpart of the bit. Like a bit, a qubit has two states: 0 and 1. But here's the twist: thanks to the strange character of quantum mechanics, a qubit doesn't have to be entirely 0 or 1. Instead, it can live in a mix, or superposition, of both states concurrently (or more precisely in some position between them). Imagine a spinning coin in midair; until it lands, it's not precisely heads or tails. It captures the possibility for both results while it whirls. A qubit in superposition can likewise represent 0, 1, or any probability-weighted mix of the two. This capacity to live in several states at once opens a world of possibilities beyond what classical bits can accomplish.

Bit

Classical computing

Qubit

Quantum computing

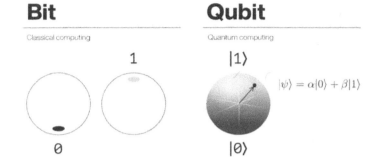

Figure 1: Two potential states—zero and one—represented as points define classical bits. Represented as the surface of a sphere (the Bloch sphere), a continuum of possible states, qubits are a superposition of zero and one. Source: https://resources.mouser.com/methods/engineering-the-quantum-future

When analyzing problem-solving, one can better understand the superposition power of a qubit. Every bit in classical computing contributes a single binary state at any one moment, so addressing issues usually calls for sequential or restricted parallelism evaluation of options. For instance, three classical bits can represent any one of eight combinations—000, 001, 010, and so on—although only one at a time. Thanks to superposition, a three-qubit quantum system can concurrently represent all eight configurations. The difference between both representations grows exponentially when adding more qubits. Ten qubits concurrently represent all 1,024 possible states at once; ten classical bits offer a glimpse of one of the 1,024 possible states at a time.

While superposition lets one qubit explore several states concurrently, the qubits' entanglement represents a key feature of quantum computing. Entanglement is the phenomenon wherein two or more qubits are coupled such that, independent of their physical distance, the state of one qubit is exactly dependent on the state of the other. Although it might sound too far-fetched, entanglement has been experimentally confirmed countless times and is the cornerstone of quantum computing.

To better understand entanglement, consider a pair of gloves. When you discover one glove in a drawer, you automatically become aware of the color and type of its counterpart, wherever it might be; even if the second glove is on the other side of the house. Qubits, however, have a crucial twist: the link between them isn't based on predetermined properties. The same idea stands for entangled qubits. Their states are linked in a way that entanglement only reveals itself when one of them is measured. If one qubit is in state 0, its entangled partner will instantly adopt the complementary state even if it's miles—or theoretically light-years—away.

This unique feature has a major effect on computing. Bits in a classical computer are independent entities; altering the state of one bit does not change the others. On a quantum computer, however, entangled qubits function as a single system that allows them to coordinate their states and operations in ways far more effective. By processing data collectively instead of separately, quantum computers can solve problems that are unreachable for their conventional equivalents.

Superposition with entanglement gives quantum computers their special advantage. While entanglement guarantees that these options are tightly linked, superposition allows qubits to represent several possibilities concurrently. Collectively, they create a computational framework capable of exploring large solution areas, optimizing challenging systems, and simulating events completely out of reach for classical systems. For drug research, for instance, challenges like simulating chemical interactions or optimizing supply chains with many variables may become feasible with quantum computing, instead of the theoretical daydreams they represent in the classical paradigm (depending on the complexity and the size of the problem).

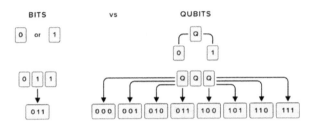

Figure 2: Comparison of classical bits and qubits: Bits represent a single state (0 or 1), while qubits leverage superposition to represent all possible states simultaneously. Source: https://inlab.fib.upc.edu/es/uncategorized-ca-es/que-puede-aportar-la-fisica-cuantica-la-computacion/2021/

Should this all still seem a little abstract or far-fetched, don't worry. Throughout the book, as we dig further into quantum algorithms, the advantages of entanglement will become more obvious. For now, it's sufficient to understand that entanglement transforms qubits into so much more than just building blocks—they become a tightly linked team, able to pull off feats beyond any bit's wildest dreams.

Future power

After we have established the basis with superposition and entanglement, let's investigate how these features become the bedrock of quantum computing's capabilities and advantages. Understanding this can help one decipher why qubits are such a big promise in certain tasks, where they outmatch conventional bits substantially.

In classical computing, the necessary steps to process all conceivable answers usually determines the speed and efficiency of problem solving. Consider this example: breaking a password composed only by letters. To finally get the right password, a classical computer must try every conceivable combination of characters one by one—or with some clever optimizations, in parallel. The classical computer must assess up to 26^8 combinations if the password consists of eight characters, each of which can be one of 26 letters. This takes time—even on a powerful computer.

On the other hand, by leveraging qubits in superposition and entanglement, a quantum computer can explore multiple possibilities simultaneously. This capability allows quantum algorithms, such as Grover's algorithm, to find the correct solution much more efficiently than a classical approach, which would require checking each possibility one by one. Specifically, Grover's algorithm reduces the number of steps needed to search an unsorted database from a linear scale to a square-root scale relative to the total number of choices. This significant reduction in computational steps is why quantum computing is often described as providing a "speedup" for certain types of problems.

Quantum speedup goes beyond these basic examples. Think about optimization problems, including financial portfolio design, supply chain management, and aircraft scheduling. To identify the most effective answer, these challenges require the analysis of millions of variables and restrictions. Classical computers struggle with these problems since the time needed to assess all possible combinations increases exponentially as the solution space gets more complex. Quantum computers, however, can substantially reduce computing times by using the linked character of entangled qubits to simultaneously handle several variables.

Machine learning is one of the most promising applications of quantum computing, as both fields aim to uncover patterns in large-scale data. Classical machine learning techniques excel at this task, though their effectiveness can be constrained by the complexity of the dataset and the challenge of separating nonlinearly distributed data. Quantum computers, however, can encode these datasets into quantum states, enabling algorithms to process information in fundamentally different ways—potentially capturing intricate relationships that classical methods struggle to model efficiently.

Simulating nature itself is another arena in which quantum computing excels. Many natural processes—including chemical reactions, protein folding, or the behavior of quantum materials—are intrinsically quantum in character. Classical computers find it difficult to replicate these systems precisely since their approximation of quantum behavior relies on an excessive consumption of computing resources. But since they run on the same principles as the systems they replicate, quantum computers are best suited for these jobs, including inventing new pharmaceuticals, materials, or even sustainable energy solutions.

Although quantum computers will probably be used alongside classical computers instead of replacing them, they are, nonetheless, significant. For many daily tasks such as word processing, video rendering, or maintaining a website, classical computers remain faster and more efficient. Quantum computers excel in solving problems that involve large solution areas, intricate interdependencies, or have inherent quantum characteristics. Therefore, with each one of them playing their part, quantum and classical systems are complementary.

The building blocks: quantum gates

Logic gates control both information flow and operations carried out on it in classical computing. These gates—AND, OR, NOT—take one or more bits as input, run them under a particular rule, and generate an output bit. A NOT gate, for example, flips a bit—a 0 becomes a 1 and a 1 becomes a 0. By means of bit manipulation, combinations of these gates enable classical computers to solve difficult problems and execute sophisticated calculations.

Gates are also used in quantum computers, but with a simple yet meaningful twist: quantum gates work on qubits. Therefore, gates not only modify the 0 or 1 state of a qubit, but also its probabilistic superposition of states. Quantum gates are characterized, theoretically, by unitary operations: essentially, transformations that retain the total probability of all conceivable states. Classical gates, instead, have set results. These gates spin, flip, or entangle qubits in ways that are simply not possible with traditional logic gates.

Among the most basic quantum gates, we find the Hadamard gate. Applied to a qubit in the state |0⟩ (read as "ket-zero"), the Hadamard gate places the qubit in a superposition of equiprobable |0⟩ and |1⟩ states. Thus, the qubit is a combination of both states instead of precisely 0 or 1. Applying the Hadamard gate to a qubit in the state |1⟩ likewise produces a superposition. This capacity to produce superpositions is essential since it sets the basis for the parallelism of quantum processing.

The Pauli-X gate is like the quantum version of a classical NOT gate—it simply flips a qubit's state. If the qubit is in |0⟩, it becomes |1⟩, and if it's in |1⟩, it switches to |0⟩. But things get more interesting when a qubit is in superposition. Instead of just swapping 0s and 1s, the Pauli-X gate also flips the "weights" of the superposition. For example, if a qubit starts as a|0⟩ + b|1⟩, applying the Pauli-X gate turns it into b|0⟩ + a|1⟩. This subtle effect highlights how quantum gates do more than just switch states—they manipulate quantum information in unique ways that classical gates can't.

In addition to controlling single qubits, quantum gates can also link multiple qubits together through entanglement. A perfect example is the CNOT gate (Controlled-NOT gate). This gate operates on two qubits: a control qubit and a target qubit. If the control qubit is in the state |1⟩, the CNOT gate flips the state of the target qubit—turning |0⟩ into |1⟩ or vice versa. However, if the control qubit is in |0⟩, the target qubit remains unchanged. This ability to create correlations between qubits is essential for quantum algorithms and is what enables quantum computers to perform operations that classical computers cannot easily replicate.

So why are quantum gates so crucial? Designed to precisely instruct qubits to generate a desired response when measured, each quantum gate is a step in a quantum algorithm. By using the ideas of superposition and entanglement, these gates allow quantum computers to do intricate transformations that solve problems in ways that classical gates cannot.

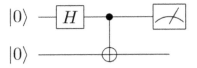

Figure 3: This figure illustrates a simple quantum circuit. The top qubit is initialized to |0⟩, passes through a Hadamard gate (H) to create superposition, and then acts as the control qubit for a CNOT gate. The circuit demonstrates the creation of an entangled Bell state. Source: https://dojo.qulacs.org/en/latest/notebooks/1.4_quantum_circuit_diagram.html

The analogy between quantum and classical gates emphasizes the essential difference between classical and quantum computation. Operating step by step to provide predictable outcomes, classical gates control deterministic binary states. Conversely, quantum gates control connected and probabilistic states; said condition usually requires meticulous coordination to guarantee the appropriate outcome when the quantum system collapses into a measurable state. This makes designing and using quantum gates both difficult and powerful.

Quantum gates are essentially our means of interacting with qubits—our language. These are the building blocks that enable us to leverage the unusual and counterintuitive actions of quantum physics and convert them into significant computations. Like a musical instrument without someone to play it, qubits' potential would stay unrealized without quantum gates.

Quantum gates, serving as the fundamental building blocks of quantum circuits that process and examine data in a unique manner, are integral to quantum machine learning algorithms. These gates allow algorithms to take advantage of the unique features of quantum systems that we mention before, like superposition, entanglement, and interference, to process data in ways that are different from traditional methods.

Quantum gates are used in quantum machine learning to encode data into quantum states, modify those states in line with a model or algorithm, and derive important insights upon state measurement. Data can be stored into qubits, for example, by initializing them into particular quantum states, and then, apply gates such as the Hadamard or Pauli gates. Once programmed, quantum gates move the qubits to carry out rotations, projections, or distance computations—similar to what classical algorithms do. Often coordinated to operate at the same time, these changes leverage quantum systems' capacities to simultaneously assess several options.

One important application of quantum gates are quantum kernels. These are often utilized in one of the most popular QML algorithms: quantum support vector machines. By creating a high-dimensional quantum feature space, quantum gates can generate intricate entangled states capturing relationships between data points. Built from sequences of quantum gates, these kernels allow quantum computers, in certain scenarios, to more effectively calculate similarities between data points compared with conventional approaches.

Likewise, building variational quantum circuits—which lie at the core of many quantum neural networks—requires quantum gates. A succession of layers of gates that parameterize the quantum state make up these circuits; these allow the model to "learn" by changing the gate parameters during training.

The application of quantum gates in machine learning transcends simple data encoding or modifications. Another key aspect of machine learning models is optimization; such procedures are often applied when training models. For a variational quantum algorithm, quantum gates are set up to create a circuit whose output molds the solution to an optimization problem. By using guided classical optimization routines, varying the values of these gates gradually enhances the performance of the quantum model by merging quantum and classical resources for effective learning.

Although this chapter explains the fundamental ideas behind quantum gates and their use in machine learning, we'll address their application in particular algorithms throughout the upcoming chapters, with a deep dive on their relevance. In them, we'll discuss how quantum circuits, with a focus on applications like classification, are built using gates. Given the current situation of quantum hardware, we'll also investigate how quantum gates interact with classical machine learning components in hybrid quantum-classical algorithms.

For now, it's enough to understand that quantum gates are the instruments enabling us to intersect the pragmatic needs of machine learning with the abstract world of quantum physics. They convert abstract ideas into practical actions, therefore opening the path for quantum systems to significantly contribute to one of the most revolutionary technologies of our time.

The well-known Bloch sphere

In quantum computing, the Bloch sphere is a useful visual aid that provides an easy approach to illustrate the state of a single qubit. Leveraging the concepts behind quantum mechanics—more especially, superposition, as it was discussed above—qubits can exist in a continuum of states, unlike classical bits, which can only occupy one of two states (0 or 1). The Bloch sphere enables us to work geometrically with these states.

Imagine a perfect sphere floating in a void with its surface representing all conceivable pure qubit states. At the zenith we find the state $|0\rangle$; at the nadir the state $|1\rangle$. Every point on the surface of this sphere represents a distinct qubit state, defined not only by its position but also by its interaction with its poles. This representation results from a qubit's inherent connection to a three-dimensional geometric structure and from its states' representation using complex numbers.

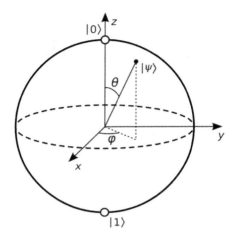

Figure 4: The Bloch sphere is a visual representation of a qubit's state in quantum mechanics, where pure states lie on the surface and mixed states inside. It shows superposition and phase using angles θ and φ. Source: https://mstale20.medium.com/basics-of-quantum-computing-with-cirq-5f77ec83e739

The Bloch sphere is beautiful in simplicity. When a qubit is in a superposition, its state resides somewhere in this sphere, not limited to the binary poles, but rather throughout a large, continuous spectrum of possibilities. The so-called pure states lie on the surface and mixed states inside. A pure state represents a quantum system in a definite quantum superposition, where we have complete information about how it was prepared—for example, an electron spin definitely pointing 30 degrees up from the horizontal. In contrast, a mixed state describes a situation where we have classical uncertainty about the quantum state—like having a 70% chance the electron was prepared spinning up and a 30% chance it was prepared spinning down. Imagine cutting through the Bloch sphere; the cross-sections expose countless paths a qubit can travel between |0⟩ and |1⟩. This makes it an essential instrument for visualizing quantum processes.

Think about how quantum gates are used. These movements on the Bloch sphere, similar to rotations or reflections, gracefully change the state of the qubit. An X (or NOT) gate, for instance, flips the qubit from |0⟩ to |1⟩ or vice versa. On the sphere, this is represented by a 180-degree turn around a given axis. More complex gates, such as the Hadamard gate, place the qubit in an equidistant combination of |0⟩ and |1⟩, therefore producing superpositions. Graphed on the Bloch sphere, this is represented by a state vector of the qubit lying midway between the poles.

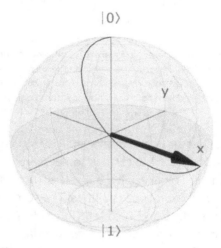

Figure 5: This figure shows what happens when we initiate a qubit in state 0 and then apply a Hadamard gate (visualizing in a Bloch sphere).

Furthermore, the Bloch sphere is also helpful in illustrating the idea of quantum measurement. Measuring a qubit forces us to project its state onto one of the axes, usually collapsing it into |0⟩ or |1⟩ following its probability's proximity to the corresponding poles. Picturing the state vector decanting to one of these two extremes in the sphere clearly demonstrates this collapse, a key concept in quantum physics.

Apart from its instructional importance, the Bloch sphere helps create and debug quantum algorithms. It enables engineers and researchers to see how operations influence qubits and guarantee circuits behave as expected. It's noteworthy, nonetheless, that the Bloch sphere is only able to represent single-qubit states. The complexity skyrockets with multi-qubit systems, which would require higher-dimensional graphics.

Further Reading

The Strange World of Quantum Mechanics:
https://www.cambridge.org/core/books/strange-world-of-quantum-mechanics/9AF95F50A66EB25B338ABB2783B9BA47

Modern Quantum Mechanics:
https://www.amazon.com/Modern-Quantum-Mechanics-J-Sa-kurai/dp/1108422411

Totally Random: Why Nobody Understands Quantum Mechanics (A Serious Comic on Entanglement):
https://press.princeton.edu/books/paperback/9780691176956/totally-random?srsltid=AfmBOooiNyUY96oXzIkxyMQzimQVxC9NhNFJgW2aKVpKw27BRXpPflhl

Quantum Physics, What Everyone Needs to Know:
https://global.oup.com/academic/product/quantum-physics-9780190250713?cc=gr&lang=en&

Quantum Computing since Democritus:
https://www.cambridge.org/core/books/quantum-computing-since-

democritus/197A4CD13738E10AAD787DBB78D8E92C#fndtn-
information

The Amazing Story of Quantum Mechanics:
https://www.amazon.com/Amazing-Story-Quantum-
Mechanics-Exploration/dp/1592406726

Introduction to Classical and Quantum Computing:
https://www.thomaswong.net/introduction-to-classical-
and-quantum-computing-1e4p.pdf

Observation of quantum entanglement with top quarks at
the ATLAS detector:
https://www.nature.com/articles/s41586-024-07824-z

Introduction to Bell's inequality in Quantum Mechanics:
https://arxiv.org/abs/2409.07597

IBM Course on Grover's Algorithm:
https://learning.quantum.ibm.com/course/fundamentals-of-
quantum-algorithms/grovers-algorithm

Quantum Cryptography Shor's Algorithm Explained:
https://www.classiq.io/insights/shors-algorithm-explained

IBM Course on Quantum Circuits:
https://learning.quantum.ibm.com/course/basics-of-quantum-
information/quantum-circuits

Chapter Figures

Figure 1: Bit vs qubit states
https://resources.mouser.com/methods/engineering-the-quantum-future

Figure 2: Bit vs qubit information
https://inlab.fib.upc.edu/es/uncategorized-ca-es/que-puede-aportar-la-fisica-cuantica-la-computacion/2021/

Figure 3: Quantum circuit
https://dojo.qulacs.org/en/latest/notebooks/1.4_quantum_circuit_diagram.html

Figure 4: The Bloch sphere
https://mstale20.medium.com/basics-of-quantum-computing-with-cirq-5f77ec83e739

Figure 5: Hadamard gate operation on the Bloch sphere
Made using the Bloch sphere simulator https://bloch.kherb.io/

CHAPTER 2

Do Quantum Computers Really Exist?

Introduction

For many, the concept of quantum computers seems almost a Star Trek piece of science fiction machinery—a concept that evokes the furthest future, alongside teleportation and flying automobiles. The interesting truth, though, is that quantum computers not only exist; they are already available in cloud services, offered by companies like Amazon and Microsoft, which have included quantum computing vendors into their technological stacks, making these machines available to academics, developers, and simply those who are brave enough to give them a try.

Along with simulators that enable users to create and test quantum algorithms, these cloud platforms provide access to genuine quantum processors—often known as Quantum Processing Units (QPUs). Thanks to this accessibility, businesses from all sizes and industries, ranging from banking to pharmaceuticals, from startups to conglomerates, can investigate the possibilities of quantum computing without having to buy or operate the technology themselves (except in a handful of cases that wealthy companies or governments manage to pay for or produce their own quantum devices).

The variety in methods used by quantum hardware providers makes this subject even more interesting. Unlike conventional computers, where silicon-based CPUs predominate, quantum computing has spawned multiple rival technologies, each with special benefits and difficulties. While some rely on superconducting qubits—which run at temperatures lower than outer space to reduce noise and guarantee stable quantum states— like IBM and Google, others, such as IonQ, apply trapped-ion technology, where individual ions are suspended and controlled by electromagnetic fields. The latter can be slower than superconducting qubits, but it achieves superior levels of accuracy.

Other players, including PsiQuantum, are investigating photonic quantum computing. Due to their room-temperature operation and well-understood optical components, photonic techniques promise scalability. Companies such as D-Wave have developed quantum annealing, a specific type of quantum computing best suited for addressing optimization issues instead of general-purpose processing.

The range of QPU designs accentuates the continuous field experimentation. Every technology represents a different way to use quantum physics for computation. Although this diversity promotes innovation, it also makes it more difficult to forecast which strategy will predominate in the future—or whether various technologies will coexist, each shining in particular use cases.

The availability of quantum computers today does not imply they are as useful or as common as their predecessors, classical computers. Often regarded as belonging in the NISQ (Noisy Intermediate-Scale Quantum) period, current quantum devices are small in scale and prone to errors, mainly due to external noise. Still, even these flawed devices are creating amazing, not-long-ago-entirely-theoretical opportunities.

We shall discuss these technologies more thoroughly in the sections that follow. We'll go over their present capabilities, working conditions, and the challenges they face as they approach their ultimate goal: being useful instruments that can address and solve practical issues better than their predecessors. First, though, let's examine closely the businesses and technologies propelling this quantum revolution.

NISQ

Physicist John Preskill first used the term NISQ in 2018 to characterize the present level of quantum computing progress. This era is defined by devices with enough qubits to investigate real quantum events. However, their size, stability, and error rates still impose major constraints. Usually running with tens to hundreds of qubits—far less than the millions required for large-scale quantum computing—these devices are known as "intermediate-scale." They are "noisy" since the quantum states and activities within them are quite sensitive to hardware faults and environmental disturbances. NISQ devices have opened the path for innovative research and early applications in optimization, machine learning, and quantum simulations, even if they are not yet able to surpass classical computers in a wider spectrum of jobs.

One of the most frequently applied technologies in NISQ devices is superconducting qubits. These qubits are produced by means of small loops of superconducting material allowing electric currents to pass unhindered. This feature lets qubits reside in superposition or entangled configurations and helps create and control quantum states. These quantum states are quite delicate, though, and to preserve their coherence, very precise environmental conditions are required. Superconducting qubits must run at temperatures close to absolute zero—usually around 15 millikelvin—which is colder than outer space. Dilution refrigerators preserve the cold environment required to stop thermal energy from disturbing the qubits, hence enabling these severe settings. Superconducting qubits are quite sensitive to noise, including physical vibrations and stray electromagnetic fields, which can disrupt their quantum states even under these conditions.

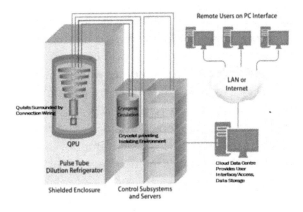

Figure 6: This representation depicts the process of executing a quantum computing task. Jobs are sent via the cloud to control and measurement systems, where microwave electronics process signals and interact with the quantum processor (an IBM superconducting one in this example). The results are digitized, classified by a classical computer, and sent back to the user over the cloud. Source: https://www.linkedin.com/pulse/raise-quantum-computing-dr-gopala-krishna-behara/

One major obstacle NISQ devices must overcome is decoherence. Decoherence is the loss of quantum characteristics of a qubit caused by interactions with its surroundings. By these means, this interaction essentially "measures" it resulting in reducing the qubit's superposition into a definite state of either 0 or 1. Coherence time is the interval in which a qubit can retain its quantum state before decoherence. Coherence periods for superconducting qubits are expressed in microseconds—a fleeting interval for computation. This restriction substantially limits the complexity and length that quantum algorithms (circuits) can have before they fall into decoherence.

Moreover, on top of this constraint, the quite-high rate of mistakes in quantum gates introduces even more difficulties to the process. Quantum gates are much less trustworthy than classical logic gates, since the latter operate with almost perfect accuracy. As computations go on, mistakes compound (due to error propagation) and it becomes challenging to run long and/or complex algorithms without incurring significant errors. The no-cloning theorem prevents quantum systems from using classical computers, which solve faults by redundancy—that is, by copying data to find and fix problems. This restriction complicates attempts to apply simple mistake correction since it's impossible to replicate an arbitrary quantum state exactly.

A theoretical solution to this dilemma is quantum error correction. In theory, systems with quantum error correction should be able to find and rectify errors without compromising the quantum information. They achieve this by embedding logical qubits (abstract, error-protected qubits that store and process the quantum information we want to use) into ensembles of physical qubits (the actual hardware qubit components that implement quantum operations but are prone to errors). Correcting mistakes for one logical qubit could require dozens or even hundreds of physical qubits, a degree of complexity that present NISQ hardware struggles to handle. Consequently, instead of obtaining actual error correction, researchers have to rely on error-mitigating strategies to reduce the effect of noise and mistakes.

Notwithstanding these constraints, the NISQ age is an essential phase of development for quantum computing. These tools allow researchers to investigate hybrid quantum-classical models, test early quantum algorithms, and find situations in which quantum computers might eventually outperform classical ones. They also provide a testing ground for hardware development, guiding researchers toward coherence times, noise reduction, and fault-tolerant quantum systems building.

Although superconducting qubits highlight the wider possibilities and difficulties of the NISQ era, these problems are not exclusive to this technology. Other QPU technologies, including but not limited to ion-trapped systems, photonic qubits, and annealers, have comparable limitations. Every method has specific benefits, but challenges in regards to noise, stability, and error correction are similar throughout all of them. The NISQ era is finally a transitional phase that will lead us towards the future, a future where fault-tolerant quantum computing is the norm, in which scalable, dependable quantum devices will unlock the full possibilities of this paradigm-shifting technology.

Superconducting

Among the most developed (and generally used) technologies in quantum computing nowadays, we can find superconducting qubits. Their scalability and rather quick gate speed—relative to other quantum technologies— make them the go-to option for many researchers and hardware developers. Several top suppliers in this industry are exploring ideas to enhance the performance, dependability, and accessibility of superconducting quantum processors. Said providers include IBM Quantum, Google Quantum AI, Rigetti Computing, and Oxford Quantum Circuits (OQC).

Built from circuits composed of superconducting materials—such as aluminum or niobium, which show negligible electrical resistance when cooled to almost absolute zero (-273 degrees Celsius)—superconducting qubits lie between two superconducting layers. These circuits have a thin insulating barrier called a Josephson junction. The Josephson junction enables the qubit to act quantum mechanically, allowing the superposition of states $|0\rangle$ and $|1\rangle$ as well as transitions between them. Using microwave pulses— for quantum gates or operations—on the qubits, the energy levels of these quantum states are precisely controlled.

IBM Quantum, a hardware and software pioneer, is one of the big players in the superconducting arena. Under the names Eagle, Falcon, and Hummingbird, IBM has continuously released quantum processors that feature rising qubit counts and connectivity. With its IBM Quantum Experience cloud system, the business has made quantum computing generally available so that customers all around the world can experiment with actual quantum hardware. Emphasizing modular scalability and incorporating innovative methods for error reduction, IBM's superconducting strategy positions the company as a leader and frontrunner in the quantum environment.

Google Quantum AI is another important player; it hit the news in 2019 when Sycamore, its 53-qubit processor, reached a critical milestone, sometimes known as quantum supremacy. In this experiment, Google showed that its quantum computer can tackle a specific problem in seconds, while it would take a classical supercomputer hundreds of years. Google's superconducting processors are well-known for their fast gate speed and high-fidelity qubits; the firm keeps extending the frontier of what is feasible with superconducting technology (including their efforts to release their last 105-qubit chip, "Willow").

Rigetti Computing, an American company specializing in quantum computing, has developed the Aspen series of quantum processors. One of Rigetti's key advancements in this area is the Aspen-M processor, a multichip quantum processor with 80 qubits. It consists of two 40-qubit chips connected using the company's proprietary multi-chip technology, designed to tackle scaling challenges in quantum computing. To support hybrid quantum software development, Rigetti has also created Forest, a quantum programming toolkit that facilitates the integration of quantum and classical workflows.

Based in the United Kingdom, Oxford Quantum Circuits (OQC) has developed a patented technology called the Coaxmon, a unique 3D architecture for superconducting qubits. Unlike traditional superconducting qubit designs, which place control and readout wiring in the same plane as the qubits, the Coaxmon moves key components off-chip into a 3D structure. This innovation simplifies fabrication, reduces interference (cross-talk) between qubits, and enhances scalability—key challenges in quantum computing.

OQC aims to build commercially viable quantum processors for industries such as finance, pharmaceuticals, and materials science. The company provides cloud-based quantum computing services, enabling businesses and researchers to access their quantum hardware remotely and apply quantum computing to real-world problems. With its novel Coaxmon design, OQC is positioning itself as a significant player in the global quantum computing landscape, contributing to the push for fault-tolerant and scalable quantum systems.

The superconducting method is attractive because it has known physics and uses existing manufacturing processes from the semiconductor industry. It faces, however, major difficulties. Superconducting qubits need temperatures close to absolute zero to operate, which requires costly and sophisticated cryogenic equipment, as mentioned above. Furthermore, the complexity needed to keep high coherence times and low error rates grows exponentially as qubit counts increase.

The competitive environment in superconducting quantum computing is accelerating development. To challenge the limits of this technology, vendors are testing creative ideas, including but not limited to new qubit designs, improved materials, and error-mitigating strategies. The endgame is to go beyond noisy, intermediate-scale devices and land fault-tolerant systems, which are able to consistently run long and sophisticated quantum algorithms.

Early on in the evolution of quantum computing, this technology stands out due to its quick gate operations and seamless integration with existing infrastructure. These players are expected to improve this technology even further in the upcoming years and therefore approach the materialization of useful, large-scale quantum systems.

Annealers

D-Wave Systems is the frontrunner in the alternative field within quantum computation that annealers represent. Unlike the gate-based quantum computers we have explored so far, annealers are not meant to be universal quantum computers. Instead, they aim to become "experts" in optimizing a specific kind of problem. Quantum annealing differs from the gate-based method used by devices like superconducting qubits or trapped ions in that it has a more limited computational intent.

Quantum annealing is based on the principle that quantum systems naturally tend to settle into their lowest-energy configuration, known as the ground state. Built to encode optimization problems into a network of qubits and their interactions, D-Wave's processors reflect a mathematical model known as a QUBO (Quadratic Unconstrained Binary Optimization) problem. After initializing its qubits in a super-position state, the quantum annealer gradually adjusts their energy landscape through a process called annealing. As this process unfolds, the qubits evolve toward a configuration that represents the optimal or near-optimal solution to the encoded problem.

D-Wave's quantum annealers and universal quantum computers have a significant difference since the first ones lack quantum gates. In a gate-based quantum computer, algorithms run as sequences of gates precisely altering qubits. Conversely, annealers do not use gates to run calculations. Rather, their qubits are under collective control via quantum tunneling and superposition, which allows them to rehearse several potential answers concurrently. For some use cases, this enables annealers to solve optimization challenges more effectively than conventional systems. However, it also reduces their applicability to a wider spectrum of computing activities.

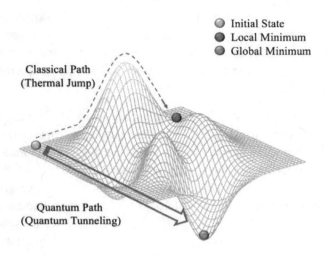

Figure 7: This figure illustrates optimization paths: the classical path (thermal jump) climbs over barriers to escape local minima, while the quantum path (quantum tunneling) leverages quantum mechanics to tunnel through barriers, reaching the global minimum more efficiently. Source: https://www.researchgate.net/publication/385352044_Evaluating_the_Ad vantage_2_Quantum_Annealer_Prototype_A_Comparative_Evaluation_wit h_Advantage_1_and_Hybrid_Solver_and_Classical_Restricted_Boltzmann_ Machines_on_MNIST_Classification

Although D-Wave's technology uses superconducting qubits, their design and operation differ from those of gate-based systems, such as those found in IBM's or Google's processors. Depending on the hardware generation, the qubits in a D-Wave system are coupled in a fixed, sparse network, generating what is known as a Chimera or Pegasus topology. These interactions determine the qubits' relationships. While this fixed architecture simplifies the hardware design, it also limits the types of problems it can express effectively.

Although they are not universal quantum computers, quantum annealers shine in specific fields where optimization is very essential. These include scheduling, financial portfolio optimization, logistics, and machine learning chores, like feature selection or clustering. A D-Wave machine might be used, for instance, by a logistics company to reduce delivery times by optimizing its delivery routes or by a financial institution to determine the most profitable combination of assets for an investment portfolio.

Quantum annealing is not without restrictions, though. Annealers cannot run arbitrary quantum algorithms, such as Shor's or Grover's, which are basic for universal quantum computing. Annealers' solutions are also not necessarily guaranteed to be exact; rather, they often generate good approximations instead of conclusive answers.

By enhancing the connection of their qubit networks and raising the accuracy with which interactions can be managed, D-Wave has solved some of these restrictions. Built with thousands of connections and improved qubits, their most recent system—the D-Wave Advantage—unlocked the encoding and solving of increasingly difficult challenges. Moreover, via its cloud platform, D-Wave offers hybrid quantum-classical solutions, therefore enabling customers to combine the advantages of quantum annealing with conventional optimization methods.

QPUs: here, there, and everywhere

Beyond superconducting qubits and quantum annealers, several other quantum computing technologies are rapidly advancing, particularly neutral atoms, trapped ions, and photonic quantum computing. Each of these approaches offers unique advantages for processing quantum information, making them attractive to companies striving to develop scalable and reliable quantum systems. While their underlying techniques differ—ranging from manipulating individual atoms with lasers to encoding quantum states in light—their common goal is to harness the power of quantum mechanics to revolutionize computing.

In neutral atom quantum computing, individual atoms kept in place by properly targeted laser beams create optical traps that generate qubits. Laser pulses enable manipulation of these atoms to encode and process data. The employment of highly excited states, sometimes referred to as Rydberg states, which enable strong interactions between adjacent atoms, is unique to neutral atoms. These interactions allow multi-qubit gates and entanglement, a cornerstone for quantum algorithms. One of the main advantages of neutral atom systems is their scalability; extra qubits can be incorporated into the system by adding more optical traps. Moreover, these systems run at ambient temperature, therefore avoiding the enormous cooling needs of superconducting technologies. Leading companies in this technology are Pasqal, QuEra Computing, and ColdQuanta. They all offer highly sophisticated quantum platforms, in which they harness the natural scalability and adaptability of neutral atoms.

On the other hand, trapped-ion quantum computing employs ions—charged atoms—as qubits. These ions are trapped in electromagnetic fields where laser or microwave radiation can regulate their quantum states. The stability of ions' energy levels enables exact operations and lengthy coherence periods. Thus, it has become one of the most precise quantum computing technologies as of today, mainly due to its homogeneity. Scalability is still a challenge, though, since managing multiple ions in a single trap becomes increasingly difficult. Important companies in this field are: IonQ, who has created high-fidelity trapped ion processors that are available in the cloud; and Quantinuum, a firm founded by Honeywell Quantum Solutions and Cambridge Quantum with the key objective of achieving hardware and software integration.

Finally, leveraging photons, or light particles, photonic quantum computing offers yet another potential solution. Optical components include beam splitters, waveguides, and detectors to help control photons; their quantum states are encoded in terms of polarization or phase. Since photons are intrinsically strong against decoherence, photonic devices are robust and able to operate at room temperature. Furthermore, integrated with current fiber-optic networks, photonic quantum computers represent a great promise for quantum communication and networking use cases. Pioneers in this discipline are innovation-first companies, such as PsiQuantum, Xanadu, QCI, and QuiX Quantum. While Xanadu has built the Borealis processor, pushing forward quantum machine learning and simulation, and most recently Aurora, the world's first scalable, networked quantum computer, PsiQuantum aims to build large-scale fault-tolerant quantum computers using silicon photonics and current semiconductor fabrication techniques.

With neutral atoms providing natural scalability, trapped ions shining in accuracy and coherence, and photonics using the benefits of light for networking and communication, each technology has found its niche. Altogether, they paint a rich and varied canvas of quantum innovation.

Qubit Type	Pros/Cons	Select Players
Superconducting	**Pros**: High gate speeds and fidelities. Can leverage standard lithographic processes. Among first qubit modalities so has a head start.	rigetti Google IBM Q QuTech OQC IQM qci Quantum Circuits, Inc. 本源量子 Origin Quantum
	Cons: Requires cryogenic cooling; short coherence times; microwave interconnect frequencies still not well understood.	
Trapped Ions	**Pros**: Extremely high gate fidelities and long coherence times. Extreme cryogenic cooling not required. Ions are perfect and consistent.	IONQ AQT QUANTINUUM oxford ionics Universal Quantum
	Cons: Slow gate times/operations and low connectivity between qubits. Lasers hard to align and scale. Ultra-high vacuum required. Ion charges may restrict scalability.	
Photonics	**Pros**: Extremely fast gate speeds and promising fidelities. No cryogenics or vacuums required. Small overall footprint. Can leverage existing CMOS fabs.	Ψ PsiQuantum XANADU QuiX QUANTUM ORCA Computing
	Cons: Noise from photon loss; each program requires its own chip. Photons don't naturally interact so 2Q gate challenges.	
Neutral Atoms	**Pros**: Long coherence times. Atoms are perfect and consistent. Strong connectivity, including more than 2Q. External cryogenics not required.	ColdQuanta QuEra COMPUTING INC. atom computing PASQAL
	Cons: Requires ultra-high vacuums. Laser scaling challenging.	
Silicon Spin/Quantum Dots	**Pros**: Leverages existing semiconductor technology. Strong gate fidelities and speeds.	intel Silicon Quantum Computing diraq QUANTUM MOTION QUANTUM BRILLIANCE
	Cons: Requires cryogenics. Only a few entangled gates to-date with low coherence times. Interference/cross-talk challenges.	

Figure 8: This table summarizes some of the most relevant players up to 2022 in the industry related to qubit types. Nowadays, all of them stay active, plus other newcomers in the QPU ecosystem. Source: https://medium.com/@russfein/quantum-computing-modalities-a-qubit-primer-revisited-e4382e8d4072

Although these three techniques currently dominate the field of non-superconducting quantum technology, other approaches are also under development. Aiming for fully fault-tolerant quantum computers, Microsoft is working on topological qubits, which rely on exotic quasiparticles called

Majorana fermions. Unlike most particles, which have distinct counterparts called antiparticles, Majorana fermions are unique because they act as their own antiparticles. This unusual property allows them to store quantum information in a way that is spread out and less vulnerable to errors, making them a promising path toward more stable quantum computation. Meanwhile, companies like Intel are exploring spin qubits, which utilize the spin of electrons in silicon and have the potential to integrate well with conventional semiconductor manufacturing. Although these technologies are in earlier stages compared to neutral atoms, trapped ions, and photonics, they represent exciting frontiers in the quest for practical quantum computing.

This variety of techniques emphasizes the field's fluid nature. Every technology has its own advantages and drawbacks; some shine in scalability, some in stability, and others in adaptability to current infrastructure. Whether one will eventually dominate or numerous will coexist, each customized to certain applications, remains one of the most fascinating puzzles in the ongoing race to achieve the full promise of quantum computing.

Your cloud might be a quantum cloud already

Cloud platforms have evolved into a gateway to quantum computing, granting academics, developers, and companies access to state-of-the-art quantum computers. Thanks to cloud-based services such as Amazon Braket and Microsoft Azure Quantum, anyone with an internet connection (and a bit of money) can delve into quantum computing. These systems create a setting where users can conduct simulations, test quantum algorithms, and even run programs on actual quantum hardware—all without owning or maintaining costly quantum equipment.

Integrated into the AWS ecosystem, Amazon Braket is a completely managed quantum computing tool. It lets users create and test quantum algorithms on a single interface, supporting both quantum hardware and classical simulators. Braket's multi-vendor approach, which provides access to quantum computers from several hardware manufacturers, is among its strongest points. These comprise trapped ion systems from IonQ and superconducting qubits from Rigetti. Whether it's general-purpose computation, high-precision simulations, or optimization issues, the range of hardware options lets customers select the most suitable technology for their specific needs. Braket also features a classical simulator, which becomes particularly helpful for developing and testing quantum circuits before running them on real-world hardware.

For those acquainted with AWS, using Braket is easy. Using the Braket SDK, developers may create quantum programs in Python, send jobs directly from their environment, and track their execution and outcomes using the AWS Management Console. Combining quantum and classical resources is also possible and fairly easy to accomplish, mainly using other AWS services such as S3 for data storage and SageMaker for machine learning. A user might, for instance, train a classical model on SageMaker and then fine-tune it on Braket using quantum-enhanced methods.

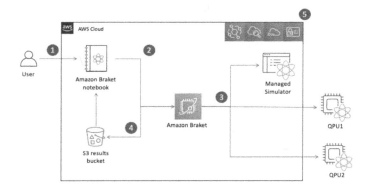

Figure 9: Amazon Braket allows you to define, submit, and monitor quantum tasks using Jupyter notebooks or the Braket SDK, with access to various QPUs, simulators, and AWS services. Results are stored in Amazon S3, with integration for IAM, CloudWatch, CloudTrail, and EventBridge for management and monitoring. Source: https://docs.aws.amazon.com/braket/latest/developerguide/braket-how-it-works.html

Although it has a somewhat different approach, Microsoft Azure Quantum presents a similarly strong solution for quantum exploration. Included in the larger Azure ecosystem, it offers powerful simulators for prototyping and access to quantum computers from companies such as IonQ, Pascal, Quantinuum, and Rigetti. Offering top-notch workflows combining the best of both computer realms, Azure Quantum is distinguished for its dedication to a hybrid quantum-classical approach. Using tools like the Q# programming language developers may create quantum applications and leverage Azure's large classical computing infrastructure to boost quantum calculations.

Both Azure Quantum and Amazon Braket remove most of the complexity associated with quantum technology. These platforms focus on usability and accessibility, offering programming environments, sample code, and thorough documentation. Braket, for example, features pre-built exa-mple notebooks; Azure Quantum offers learning modules and connectivity with widely used programming tools such as Jupyter Notebooks and Visual Studio Code.

The hardware availability in these systems is also note-worthy. Amazon Braket users may opt for IonQ's trapped ion systems for general-purpose quantum computing with high coherence times, while also using Rigetti's superconducting qubits for rapid gate-based operations. Likewise, Azure Quantum provides access to Quantinuum, IonQ, and Rigetti, alongside quantum-inspired solutions for customers looking for hybrid approaches.

The commercialization and accessibility of quantum compu-ting rely heavily on its availability via the cloud. Users of platforms like Amazon Braket and Azure Quantum can easily include quantum capabilities into their current processes and test several quantum technologies, therefore preparing themselves for the time when quantum computing becomes essential in addressing difficult issues in real-world scena-rios.

Simulation and emulation

By allowing developers to test and improve quantum algo-rithms before running them on actual quantum hardware, simulators and emulators have become absolutely vital for quantum computing. Although they are sometimes used indistinctively, these terms represent different ways to replicate quantum activity. Anyone aspiring to work in the quantum realm must first understand the differences bet-ween simulators and emulators as well as their availability from different suppliers and on cloud platforms.

A quantum simulator is a conventional computational tool modeled by mathematical approaches to replicate the behavior of quantum systems. These simulators are perfect for investigating the theoretical sides of quantum computing, since they are not hampered by the practical quantum hardware constraints like noise or limited coherence time. Simulators can replicate small to medium-sized quantum systems with great precision. Their scalability is, however, limited since the required processing resources grow exponentially for every additional simulated qubit. Simulators are the go-to option for researchers prototyping quantum algorithms, investigating quantum events, and verifying theoretical results.

By contrast, a quantum emulator aims to replicate the behavior of quantum hardware—including its flaws. Emulators replicate actual programs running on real-world quantum devices by including reasonable noise models and other limitations. This makes them useful for accounting for the noise and error rates that define present NISQ devices and, hence, test how algorithms will behave in reality. Emulators enable engineers to develop algorithms to later be tested on actual quantum processors by offering more realistic environments.

Simulation and emulation tools are relatively easily available through cloud platforms such as Amazon Braket, Azure Quantum, and IBM Quantum. The Braket simulators, for example, supports efficiently near to 24 qubits on classical resources. Each simulator is firmly linked into the Braket ecosystem and offers rapid and reliable results for smaller-scale testing, therefore facilitating smooth transitions between simulation and real hardware. For more thorough testing, Braket provides noise models that replicate the behavior of certain quantum hardware. This allows developers to optimize their algorithms before deploying them on real quantum hardware.

Leveraging the high-performance computing capabilities already available in the Azure ecosystem, Microsoft Azure Quantum offers the Quantum Development Kit (QDK), which includes a built-in quantum simulator (sparse simulator) that can be triggered on a regular laptop and even more in powerful systems. Azure also provides additional tools, such as the resource estimator, which allows noise-aware emulation users to forecast the resource needs of their quantum algorithms. Azure Quantum is a great solution for developers focusing on hybrid workflows and practical deployment scenarios.

Via its Qiskit architecture, IBM Quantum offers a broad ecosystem of simulators. By means of the Qiskit Aer Simulator, IBM's customers can replicate (depending on the Qiskit version and whether it's running locally or not) quantum circuits using noise models that mimic IBM's superconducting qubits' behavior. It's a potent instrument for realistic algorithm testing, since it includes sophisticated capabilities like adjustable noise channels.

Simulators and emulators differ primarily in their purpose: simulators focus on achieving high accuracy by simulating idealized quantum systems, whereas emulators stress real scenarios by incorporating the hardware's intrinsic flaws. These have become essential for the quantum computing process since they allow users to build, test, and improve algorithms before devoting significant time and money to real quantum devices. The availability of these tools from various suppliers and on major cloud platforms provides developers with the processing power they require, regardless of their particular use case or hardware preferences.

Simulators and emulators will become even more relevant as quantum computing develops, since they help to narrow down the theory-practice gap. They provide a risk-free testing environment, allowing researchers and developers to explore the limits of quantum processing and prepare for the eventual implementation of fault-tolerant quantum systems.

Further Reading

Quantum Excellence:
https://www.amazon.com/Quantum-Excellence-Companies-Transformational-Technology/dp/1989478182

Machine Learning with Quantum Computers:
https://www.amazon.com/Machine-Learning-with-Quantum-Computers-_Quantum-Science-and-Technology_/dp/3030830977

Quantum Computation and Quantum Information:
https://michaelnielsen.org/qcqi/QINFO-book-nielsen-and-chuang-toc-and-chapter1-nov00.pdf

Quantum Computing for Computer Scientists:
https://www.cambridge.org/core/books/quantum-computing-for-computer-scientists/8AEA723BEE5CC9F5C03FDD4BA850C711

An Introduction to Quantum Computing:
https://global.oup.com/academic/product/an-introduction-to-quantum-computing-9780198570493?cc=gr&lang=en&

Dancing with Qubits:
https://www.amazon.com/Dancing-Qubits-quantum-computing-change/dp/1838827366

Hardware Architecture for a Quantum Computer Trusted Execution Environment:
https://arxiv.org/abs/2308.03897

Quantum Computing in the NISQ era and beyond:
https://arxiv.org/abs/1801.00862

No-Cloning Theorem:
https://www.quera.com/glossary/no-cloning-theorem

Study of Decoherence in Quantum Computers: A Circuit-Design Perspective:
https://arxiv.org/abs/1904.04323

Logical Qubit:
https://www.quera.com/glossary/logical-qubit

Computing with error-corrected quantum computers:
https://www.ibm.com/quantum/blog/qldpc-codes

Introduction to quantum error correction:
https://learn.microsoft.com/en-us/azure/quantum/concepts-error-correction

Josephson junctions, superconducting circuits, and qubit for quantum technologies:
https://arxiv.org/abs/2405.20911

Technology for the quantum future by IBM:
https://www.ibm.com/quantum/technology

Rigetti quantum cloud services:
https://docs.rigetti.com/qcs

The Coaxmon by OQC:
https://oqc.tech/tech/coaxmon/

What is Quantum Annealing?:
https://docs.dwavesys.com/docs/latest/c_gs_2.html

Multiverse Computing: Optimizing Financial Portfolios with Quantum Computing:
https://www.dwavesys.com/media/5qahck2o/multiverse_case_study_v8.pdf

Quantum computing with neutral atoms:
https://arxiv.org/abs/2006.12326

Trapped ion quantum computers:
https://pennylane.ai/qml/demos/tutorial_trapped_ions

Photonic quantum computers:
https://pennylane.ai/qml/demos/tutorial_photonics

Beating classical computers with Borealis:
https://www.xanadu.ai/blog/beating-classical-computers-with-Borealis

Introducing Aurora: First modular, scalable and networked quantum computer:
https://www.youtube.com/watch?v=z0hSw2BC4mI&t=124s

Meet Willow, our state-of-the-art quantum chip:
https://blog.google/technology/research/google-willow-quantum-chip/

Azure Quantum on building scalable topological qubits:
https://news.microsoft.com/source/features/innovation/azure-quantum-majorana-topological-qubit/

Interferometric single-shot parity measurement in InAs–Al hybrid devices:
https://www.nature.com/articles/s41586-024-08445-2

Intel Takes Next Step Toward Building Scalable Silicon-Based Quantum Processors:
https://newsroom.intel.com/new-technologies/intel-quantum-research-published-in-nature

Amazon Braket Features:
https://aws.amazon.com/braket/features/

Chapter Figures

Figure 6: Executing a quantum computing task
https://www.linkedin.com/pulse/raise-quantum-computing-dr-gopala-krishna-behara/

Figure 7: Classical vs quantum path
https://www.researchgate.net/publication/385352044_Evaluating_the_Advantage_2_Quantum_Annealer_Prototype_A_Comparative_Evaluation_with_Advantage_1_and_Hybrid_Solver_and_Classical_Restricted_Boltzmann_Machines_on_MNIST_Classification

Figure 8: Summary of quantum computing approaches and companies
https://medium.com/@russfein/quantum-computing-modalities-a-qubit-primer-revisited-e4382e8d4072

Figure 9: Amazon Braket workflow
https://docs.aws.amazon.com/braket/latest/developerguide/braket-how-it-works.html

CHAPTER 3

It's Not Trivial to Pick a QPU

Introduction

Among the most important—and difficult—decisions on the quantum computing path is the selection of the appropriate Quantum Processing Unit (QPU) for a specific job or exploration. The choice of a QPU determines not only the feasibility but also the efficiency and precision of a quantum solution, much like choosing the correct tool can define the success or failure of a project. Built on several technological bases—such as superconducting circuits, trapped ions, neutral atoms, or quantum annealers, each having advantages and drawbacks—one option can be more suitable for the problem you want to solve than others. This variability, while fascinating, suggests that there is no universally applicable solution yet. The type of the problem, the intended results, and the restrictions of the use case all significantly affect the ideal QPU choice.

This chapter investigates the reasons why choosing the correct QPU is far from being meaningless. From finance to logistics, from optimization to machine learning, and from data to QPU, the effectiveness of a QPU varies considerably across sectors and applications. Quantum annealing, for example, is the go-to option when addressing combinatorial optimization problems where the interactions between variables are strongly interconnected, as we have observed at the Port of Los Angeles optimization problem (which was solved using D-Wave's annealers). On the other hand, neutral atom systems, such as those created by QuEra, are especially suited for activities like reservoir computing or quantum machine learning where adaptability and scalability are fundamental, since they are able to scale to hundreds of qubits. Conversely, superconducting qubit systems—like IBM's approach—balance programmability and performance, providing strong platforms for hybrid quantum-classical approaches, including quantum kernel applications in financial categorization problems.

Beyond the technical requirements, pragmatic factors also influence the already-complex QPU selection process. While the availability of cloud access or on-site deployment might define the accessibility of these systems for particular companies, error rates, scalability, gate fidelities, and hardware noise affect the dependability of quantum computing. For instance, the Port of Los Angeles was able to attain quantum-driven efficiency advantages without creating in-house quantum infrastructure by means of D-Wave's quantum annealers, which are available via cloud. Similarly, IBM's cloud-connected quantum processors allowed HSBC to explore Quantum Multiple Kernel Learning (QMKL), using datasets related to credit scoring and fraud detection, thereby bridging the gap between innovative research and practical application.

We'll explore the subtleties of choosing a QPU throughout this chapter, not just from a technological standpoint but also from a larger perspective, considering multiple angles, such as data compatibility and organizational goals. Although quantum computing has a universal promise, its path to realization is anything but simple. Choosing the correct QPU is as much about knowledge of the problem as it's about knowledge of the technology, whether that means maximizing shipping logistics, spotting fraudulent activity, or investigating new materials. Choosing the correct QPU requires aligning the project requirements with the capacity of a specific quantum processor. By the end of this chapter, you will understand why selecting a QPU is more art than science and why this choice can make all the difference in your quantum projects.

IonQ and the challenge of classifying images

Particularly suited for QML, IonQ's approach to quantum hardware and software is unique. To understand why their technology is one of a kind, we'll delve into their cooperation with Hyundai in an effort to leverage image recognition for self-driving cars. Real-time recognition and interpretation of a wide variety of traffic signs and road conditions represent a significant challenge for self-driving cars. With more than 500 official road signs in the United States alone, these vehicles have to be extremely accurate to guarantee dependability and safety. Though strong, classical machine learning systems can find it difficult to scale and operate with the efficiency needed for such challenging jobs. IonQ's quantum systems provide a quite different approach to address these difficulties.

IonQ's advantage stems mostly from their trapped-ion quantum computing design, which uses qubit entanglement to allow exponential scaling. These systems let each extra qubit double the computational data space, therefore enabling quantum models to easily manage vast and complicated datasets. Eight qubits, for instance, are enough to depict a sixteen by sixteen-pixel image; twenty-four qubits may encode an image with more than sixteen million pixels. Working with high-quality photographs or big datasets becomes feasible since this technology offers exponential scalability without an equivalent increase in computer resources. Applications like self-driving cars require such capabilities: achieving acceptable levels of performance in different and ever-changing environments demands increased resolution and wider coverage, something classical machine learning struggles to do.

Figure 10: Example of how a high-resolution image can go through a reduced one to be processed with 8 qubits from the IonQ device. Source: https://youtu.be/jGXTgNmPkps?si=Q4EJyRcotWMq41eU

IonQ's systems' capacity for effective data representation is another vital capability. Superposition allows quantum computers to store images efficiently by successfully compressing them into a few qubits while maintaining important details. This makes more compact and economical models possible, completely out of reach for conventional systems. Furthermore, quantum entanglement enables parallel data transformation throughout the whole dataset, therefore allowing simultaneous changes and optimization across all the pixels in an image. The training process is significantly accelerated by this natural parallelism, which is substantially more efficient than the sequential or batch processing techniques applied in traditional computing.

IonQ's quantum systems further simplify the optimization process and cut computation time by requiring fewer input parameters to adequately train models. IonQ's systems converge on highly performing models with less iterations by effectively scanning the parameter space. Smaller, more interpretable models are produced while also saving time. Furthermore, by providing a richer understanding of data and more solid models, quantum computers allow completely new types of transformations. These special transformations allow IonQ's quantum systems to find patterns and characteristics in images that classical methods could overlook, hence improving model performance.

IonQ field-tested these abilities in a collaboration with Hyundai. Hyundai's image recognition models grew faster and more flexible by using quantum computing, therefore enhancing their capacity to recognize road signs, even in challenging environments, such as poorly lit streets or damaged signs. This flexibility and IonQ's precise scalability to fit higher-resolution photos highlight the useful advantages that quantum computing has for self-driving technologies. By making autonomous cars more responsive and precise, these developments could significantly lower the computational cost of training and deploying models. In a field as sensitive as self-driving automobiles, these improvements could represent the difference between a tragedy and a prevented accident.

This technology has possibilities reaching far beyond transportation. Quantum machine learning could examine high-dimensional medical imaging data to produce faster and more accurate diagnosis. In farming, it could spot problems with crop health from satellite photos. Retail and logistics industries could maximize warehouse operations via improved object recognition. Security and military forces could use quantum technologies to detect threats in real time through superior picture and/or video analysis. And the list goes on.

IonQ's capacity to scale efficiently based on the trapped-ion technology, without depending on exponential increases in computer resources, positions it as a groundbreaking player in the field of artificial intelligence, as industries seek bigger and more complex machine learning models.

IonQ has produced 36 high-performance qubits, allowing quantum computers to outperform classical methods for particular image recognition challenges. These systems, scaled to 64 qubits (their next device), should produce outcomes in a variety of applications that surpass conventional machine learning systems. IonQ's initiatives show how quantum computing is already revolutionizing sectors and redefining what is feasible in machine learning, therefore showing present-day advantages rather than only theoretical ideals and future promises.

QuEra's disruptive approach

Leading proponent of neutral atom quantum computing—a novel method with special advantages for QML—QuEra Computing is using individually controlled atoms set in programmable lattices; their neutral atom systems achieve unmatched scalability, versatility, and programmability. QuEra's devices can control a few hundred qubits with perfect homogeneity and run at room temperature, unlike superconducting quantum computing systems. Their machines are very dependable and efficient for large-scale quantum calculations.

Among the notable applications of QuEra's technology, their work on Quantum Reservoir Computing (QRC), a fresh method for QML, stands out. Before doing lightweight classical post-processing, QRC converts classical data into quantum states so the quantum system may process information by its inherent dynamics. This approach eliminates many of the optimization issues, including hardware noise-induced mistakes and barren plateaus that exist in variational quantum algorithms. Instead, QRC relies on the inherent complexity of quantum dynamics, therefore avoiding the need for rigorous parameter optimization while preserving scalability and accuracy.

QuEra's method is most interesting when applied on their Aquila system, which is presently hosted on AWS Braket. One important demonstration included MNIST dataset handwritten digit classification. With their neutral atom hardware, QuEra converted the dataset into quantum states and obtained competitive performance, matching conventional techniques like neural networks. Running these trials on 108 qubits—the biggest quantum machine learning experiment ever conducted—QuEra proved the scalability and efficiency of their method. Since their results with this limited sample size approximated the performance of classical neural networks, future developments with more qubits and higher sampling rates look really promising.

QuEra also highlighted the possibility for relative quantum kernel advantage, a crucial first step toward reaching quantum advantage in real-world applications. Using quantum kernels to process data geometries in ways traditional systems cannot, they demonstrated that on specially tailored datasets QRC might outperform classical approaches. This sets the road ahead where quantum systems will be able to address computationally difficult issues for classical systems, particularly in fields like material science and medicine.

QuEra also used their QRC model on a variety of datasets, including image-based classifications and time-series prediction as well as defect detection in industrial processes. These tests confirmed not just QRC's adaptability but also its strength in practical environments. For the tomato leaf analysis dataset, for example, increasing the number of qubits from 9 to 108 consistently improved classification accuracy. This shows that neutral atom systems can handle problems of different sizes.

QuEra's special benefit comes from its neutral atom systems' programmability. Their hardware gives customers the liberty to adjust the technique to different kinds of data by allowing several encoding techniques like position-based or detuning-based encodings. It's possible to turn time series data into the global potential that is applied to the atoms, which turns the chaotic dynamics of a laser into predictions. This adaptability as well as the capacity to dynamically reorganize the system creates new opportunities for addressing machine learning problems.

D-Wave and the optimization issues

As strikingly shown by its use at the Port of Los Angeles, D-Wave's quantum annealing technology represents a huge leap in solving practical optimization challenges. With about 10 million twenty-foot containers handled annually, this port is the biggest in the United States. Hence, efficiency becomes the first priority. In this intricate logistical process, even little delays or inefficiencies can cause major financial losses and produce negative effects across the supply chain.

One of the most important terminals in the port, Pier 300, presented significant operational challenges in terms of the best usage of rubber-tired gantry (RTG) cranes. These large cranes carry containers set in rows across almost half a mile of yard area. Trucks arriving to pick particular containers sometimes have to wait until the required container is found and picked. The random arrangement of containers aggravates this delay, often requiring moving many obstructive containers before reaching the objective calls for cranes. Historically, the answer was to arrange cranes to fit trucks, but this method was labor-intensive and very expensive on crane resources, with poor efficiency.

Under an $850 million renovation project, the terminal's new owners hired SavantX, a firm focused on optimization technology, to solve these problems in 2018. Built on D-Wave's quantum annealing technique, SavantX created the Hyper-Optimized Nodal Efficiency Engine (HONE). This project's central innovation was the development of a digital twin—a thorough computer simulation of Pier 300's activities. Researchers analyzed more than 100,000 cargo-handling scenarios, a simulation that would be impossible to test in the real world. The HONE system was then provided with the insights from this data to identify opportunities for improvement.

D-Wave's quantum annealing method played a key role in solving the challenging scheduling issue. As the intricacy of the situation grew—especially as the number of trucks each crane could service exceeded four—traditional approaches faced considerable challenges. But quantum annealing managed the extra complexity remarkably effectively. D-Wave's quantum system kept constant performance, even when raising the number of trucks per crane to nine, unlike classical systems where computational effort increased exponentially with problem size. This capacity to scale efficiently highlighted the major benefits of quantum annealing for problems involving many linked variables and restrictions.

HONE applied at Pier 300 produced amazing results. Crane operation efficiency was one of the most notable developments. Not only did the new average and more efficient distance each crane covered—from 8,900 meters daily to 6,200 meters—save fuel and equipment, but it also let cranes finish more jobs in the same period. Crane occupancy rose from 45% to 72%; the daily delivery count increased by more than 60%, from 60 to 97. Improvements in truck turn time, which was reduced from 66 to 58 minutes, matched these operational advantages and helped to ease traffic by letting more vehicles be serviced in a given period.

Financially speaking, these tweaks had a significant effect. Tens of millions of dollars in yearly savings can result from even tiny increases in operational efficiency. Pier 300's value had tripled to $2.3 billion by 2021 when it was sold. Although other elements contributed to this increase, the quantum annealing technology of HONE and D-Wave was mostly responsible for the improved operational capacity of the terminal.

This scenario emphasizes the special advantages of D-Wave's quantum annealing technique in tackling combinatorial optimization problems—commonly found in manufacturing, supply chain management, logistics, and other sectors. Finding the best configuration or sequence of actions in systems with numerous interdependent variables and restrictions is a challenge that gets exponentially more difficult as the number of variables increases. When the problem complexity increases, classical algorithms start struggling with these tasks. By contrast, quantum annealing shines in quickly identifying high-quality solutions—even for very large-scale and highly complicated issues.

The Port of Los Angeles use case also emphasizes D-Wave's systems' adaptability. Beyond logistics, comparable quantum methods can be used in other fields, like manufacturing optimization, where resource allocation and production scheduling are major issues, or in transportation, where routing and scheduling efficiency can lower costs and increase service dependability. For example, the kind of efficiencies shown at Pier 300 are perfect for airline scheduling, urban traffic optimization, and even network design in telecoms.

The takeaways from this example go beyond simple technical mastery. The achievements at Pier 300 drove a larger awareness of quantum technology's ability to address current real-world issues—not only in the far future. D-Wave is proving that quantum computing can offer real value by concentrating on optimization issues, which are common across sectors, therefore giving early adopters a competitive edge.

IBM being tested by HSBC

By means of the creative Quantum Multiple Kernel Learning (QMKL) approach, HSBC and IBM Quantum have teamed up to show the paradigm-shifting power of quantum computing in financial applications. In the financial services sector, where effective risk classification, fraud detection, and consumer behavior modeling are vital but typically limited by the constraints of classical machine learning techniques, this cooperation tackles important difficulties. They have shown how QML can improve predictive models and get past the inherent complexity of financial datasets using IBM's quantum system.

Dealing with very complex datasets, generally marked by nonlinear correlations, high dimensionality, and structural intricacies, standard methodologies find it challenging to accurately model problems in the financial sector. By using quantum feature spaces to capture richer data linkages, quantum kernel-based approaches—including Quantum Support Vector Machines (QSVMs)—have shown promising results in solving these problems. If used in real-world quantum hardware, these methods usually suffer from exponential kernel concentration, decreased trainability, and noise-induced mistakes. Although strong in principle, single quantum kernel models sometimes fail to incorporate the many structures of financial data.

To overcome these limitations, HSBC and IBM created QMKL, a hybrid method combining several quantum kernels into one optimal composite kernel. QMKL enables flexible and strong modeling of data by linearly combining pre-defined quantum kernels and assigning weights to each kernel depending on their alignment with a target kernel. By means of these weights, a classical optimizer guarantees that the composite kernel is appropriate for the particular dataset without requiring expensive parameterized quantum circuit optimizations. Perfect for near-term quantum devices, this method reduces overfitting risk and offers resilience against noise.

The effective application of QMKL was made possible by the IBM quantum processor. Representing one of the biggest quantum kernel applications shown on real hardware, the *ibm_auckland* device permitted the execution of quantum kernels with up to 20 qubits by means of its hardware capabilities. The foundation of this success was error reduction using numerous approaches to improve performance. While pulse-efficient transpilation shortened gate execution times for two-qubit operations, ensuring that quantum circuits stayed efficient and robust, randomized compilation converted coherent noise into stochastic noise. Furthermore, error calibration methods catered kernel computations to the particular features of the quantum processor, hence preserving stability and accuracy over different qubit counts.

While several financial datasets were used to assess QMKL's performance, its results with the HSBC Digital Payment Fraud Dataset received particular attention. In terms of ROC-AUC scores, a crucial statistic for classification problems, QMKL systematically exceeded conventional kernel approaches. Particularly projected quantum kernels (PQ-MKL) showed great trainability and robustness, preserving good performance even as the feature dimension grew. This robustness was ascribed to QMKL's capacity to stabilize kernel variance and mean, hence reducing the exponential concentration problems sometimes afflicting single quantum kernels.

On the IBM quantum system, QMKL had interesting effects. Thanks to the error-mitigating process, hardware-based quantum kernels achieved near alignment with perfect simulations, even at increasing qubit counts. For up to 20 qubits, for example, projected quantum kernels showed great consistency; regression metrics like R^2 scores remained above 0.9. This stability guaranteed that models trained on the hardware could either match or surpass their classical equivalents in performance. With an average improvement of 12.5% in classification accuracy at 16 qubits, the hybrid QMKL technique notably exceeded single quantum kernel models in almost all circumstances. This emphasizes how well QMKL uses quantum technology to better address complicated financial applications.

IBM's devices' outcomes not only confirm QMKL's applicability but also its scalability and resilience under real-world conditions. QMKL established a new benchmark for quantum machine learning in the finance industry by providing consistent performance over both simulation and hardware executions. A major turning point in the path towards useful quantum computing is the ability to improve classification models using quantum kernels while guaranteeing stability and accuracy on noisy hardware.

The cooperative success of HSBC and IBM with QMKL outlines a bright future for quantum-enhanced financial modeling. These developments will be particularly helpful in credit scoring, risk classification, and fraud detection systems. QMKL's capacity to expand to bigger datasets and feature areas as quantum technology develops will increase its transforming power for the financial sector even more.

More than just the QPU brand

Beyond brand names and theoretical capabilities, choosing the correct quantum processing unit for your quantum machine learning initiatives depends, mainly, on finding the correct metrics. Researchers in QML have to evaluate QPUs from another perspective, much as traditional machine learning practitioners evaluate hardware depending on processing power, memory, and GPU capabilities. These measures directly affect the viability and efficiency of running quantum algorithms as well as their expected success rate.

Gate fidelity, which represents how precisely a QPU executes quantum operations relative to their ideal theoretical counterparts, is among the most important criteria to take into account. High gate fidelity guarantees that the outcomes of QML, where algorithms depend on exact transformations of quantum states, remain true to the intended computation. Low gate fidelity systems cause mistakes that could build up over a quantum circuit's layers and produce noisy outputs that reduce algorithm performance. When building quantum feature maps or deep variational quantum circuits, where even small variations might compromise the data representation and optimization procedures, fidelity measures become even more important.

Qubit coherence time is another crucial measurement; it describes a qubit's quantum state lifetime before decoherence or external noise results. Deep or complicated circuits in algorithms demand longer coherence times to run consistently. In this sense, trapped-ion QPUs generally outperform their superconducting counterparts, offering the stability needed for algorithms requiring continuous interaction between qubits, such as those employed in quantum kernel estimation or reinforcement learning applications.

Equally crucial is qubit connectivity, especially for methods needing large entanglement or qubit interactions. In QML experiments, the efficiency of the circuit depends on the connection and determines whether further swap operations are required to entangle far-off qubits. Inaccurate connectivity can lower general fidelity and raise circuit depth, adding noise. By reducing the demand for error-prone intermediary steps, hardware such as IonQ's trapped-ion systems—which provide all-to-all connectivity—simplifies circuit design and improves algorithm performance.

Another important factor, especially for scaling QML algorithms, is the qubit count accessible on a QPU. More complicated models or larger datasets could require more qubits to encode data or represent sophisticated patterns. But simply counting the qubits is insufficient; their quality—determined by metrics like error rates and fidelity—must also be considered. For example, even if a QPU has a large qubit count, the dependability of the calculation may decrease considerably if those qubits are noisy.

Furthermore, execution time and gate speed are also important when choosing a QPU for a QML experiment. Mostly featuring great gate speed, superconducting QPUs enable quick implementation of algorithms devoid of extended coherence durations. On the other hand, albeit slower, trapped-ion systems provide accuracy and fidelity, which makes them a better choice for studies when these supersede speed. In iterative algorithms such as variational quantum classifiers, where numerous iterations are needed to adjust parameters, balancing execution time with fidelity is critical.

One cannot overlook cost-efficiency; metrics like quantum volume offer measurements for a QPU's whole performance. Providing a high-level overview of the pragmatic utility of a system, quantum volume aggregates key elements of a quantum system, including qubits, gate integrity, coherence time, and connection into a single metric. Although it's not the only factor to take into account, quantum volume offers a reasonable basis for evaluating different QPUs in several use cases.

Ultimately, how easily a QPU may be included in your research pipeline depends on accessibility and integration criteria, such as latency in accessing cloud-based QPUs and compatibility with traditional methods. These factors can significantly affect the time and effort needed to run tests for QML practitioners who mostly depend on hybrid quantum-classical algorithms.

A QPU's specifications are not just technical details; they can easily boost or undermine the performance of your QML algorithms in production. Careful analysis of these indicators helps researchers make decisions and choose the hardware that better fits their objectives, therefore guaranteeing that their experiments are not only theoretically sound but also practically feasible.

Further Reading

IonQ and Hyundai Motor Expand Partnership to Use Quantum Computing for Object Detection:
    https://www.hyundai.com/worldwide/en/newsroom/detail/0000000050

Learn Quantum: Machine Learning Image Recognition Application:
    https://ionq.com/resources/learn-quantum-machine-learning-image-recognition-application

Aquila, QuEra's 256-qubit Analog Quantum Computer:
    https://www.quera.com/aquila

Large-scale quantum reservoir learning with an analog quantum computer:
    https://arxiv.org/abs/2407.02553

SavantX's Hone platform integrated with D-Wave's quantum annealing:
    https://www.savantx.com/hone

Quantum Annealing for Industry Applications: Introduction and Review:
    https://arxiv.org/abs/2112.07491

Quantum Multiple Kernel Learning in Financial Classification Tasks:
    https://arxiv.org/abs/2312.00260

Benchmarking Quantum Computers: Towards a Standard
Performance Evaluation Approach:
  https://arxiv.org/html/2407.10941v2

HamilToniQ: An Open-Source Benchmark Toolkit for
Quantum Computers:
  https://arxiv.org/abs/2404.13971

IonQ Aria Furthers Lead As World's Most Powerful
Quantum Computer:
  https://ionq.com/news/february-23-2022-ionq-aria-furthers-
  lead

Chapter Figures

Figure 10: Reduced-sized image for pattern recognition with
IonQ device
  https://youtu.be/jGXTgNmPkps?si=Q4EJyRcotWMq41eU

## CHAPTER 4

Implementing Quantum Machine Learning Models with Python

Introduction

Although QML promises to transform how we handle and analyze challenging datasets, using these models requires a strong knowledge of both classical and quantum programming tools. Mainly covering Python, the most flexible programming language for these two fields, this chapter will be your initial manual for configuring and navigating the fundamental technologies behind quantum machine learning.

We shall start by introducing Python, although somehow generally, so as to bridge the gap between classical and quantum computing. The fundamental libraries and frameworks underlying any machine learning process will be discussed in this part. Pandas helps with effective data manipulation; NumPy drives numerical computing with its array-handling features; and scikit-learn streamlines traditional machine learning tasks with its arsenal of simple tools. Though traditional in character, these libraries are crucial stepping stones for quantum applications. They let us construct feature transformations, preprocess data, and even assess classical baselines against which quantum methods can be measured.

Especially when switching between classical and quantum systems, organizing your programming environment might be intimidating. We'll walk you through establishing a user-friendly configuration using Anaconda, a well-known platform that simplifies the management of Python environments and dependencies, therefore helping to ease this procedure. We'll also introduce you to Jupyter Notebook, an interactive development environment that elegantly connects with both classical and quantum tools. Jupyter Notebook is the perfect tool for quantum machine learning experimentation since it allows you to write, test, and document code, all in one place.

Once you feel at ease with the traditional tools and environment configuration, we'll enter the quantum world with an emphasis on two Python-based software development kits (SDKs) that have become the frontrunners and go-to options in the field: Qiskit and PennyLane.

Developed by IBM, Qiskit is a strong and flexible framework that allows you to create and run quantum circuits as well as replicate them on real-world quantum hardware. Qiskit is an ecosystem, not simply a quantum SDK. It incorporates tools for working with quantum circuits, error-reducing strategies, and even visualization modules to assist in better understanding of quantum states. A key part of quantum machine learning, hybrid quantum-classical algorithms will be designed using Qiskit. From data encoding into quantum states, through quantum gate application to outcome measurement, Qiskit offers the means to navigate every step of your quantum workflow.

On the other corner of the quantum software ring, we find PennyLane. Designed by Xanadu, it approaches quantum computing from a different but complementary standpoint.

It centers on quantum differentiable programming, a paradigm combining backpropagation methods of machine learning with quantum mechanical ideas. PennyLane is therefore particularly strong for quantum machine learning since it lets you create and maximize quantum models straightforwardly. PennyLane closes the gap between quantum and classical systems by deftly integrating into machine learning tools such as TensorFlow and PyTorch. We'll show how this framework may be applied to create quantum neural networks and other differentiable quantum models, hence stretching the possibilities of what machine learning can accomplish.

This chapter is about arming you with the ability to handle both classical and quantum environments, not only about the tools. As a hybrid field, quantum machine learning typically hinges on how well you can combine classical preprocessing, quantum computation, and classical post-processing into a coherent pipeline. By the end of this chapter, you will not only grasp Python's classical and quantum libraries but also have the confidence to create and test your own quantum-enhanced machine learning models.

Python in a nutshell

Python is the gateway to building both classical and quantum machine learning models. In this section, we'll focus on setting up the tools and understanding the key libraries that form the backbone of classical machine learning. While we'll explore quantum frameworks like Qiskit and Pennylane later, a solid understanding of Python basics is essential for preparing data and evaluating models.

This guide walks you through setting up a clean Python environment and introduces three critical libraries: pandas,

NumPy, and scikit-learn. Along the way, we'll cover practical examples and ensure you're equipped to manipulate datasets, perform numerical computations, and build machine learning pipelines.

Setting up the environment

To begin with, you need a clean and organized environment to ensure that your work is isolated and dependencies are conflict-free. Using Anaconda, a popular Python distribution, is the easiest way to set this up.

Step 1: Download and install Anaconda

1. Visit the official Anaconda website and download the installer suitable for your operating system (Windows, macOS, or Linux).
   https://www.anaconda.com/download

2. Run the installer and follow the on-screen instructions. Make sure to add Anaconda to your system's PATH variable if prompted during installation.

Step 2: Open the Anaconda prompt

Once installed, open the Anaconda Prompt. On Windows, you can find this by searching for "Anaconda Prompt" in the Start menu. On macOS or Linux, simply open your terminal.

Step 3: Create a new environment

With the Anaconda Prompt or terminal open, create a dedicated Python environment for this project by typing:

```
conda create --name qml_env python=3.9
```

- `qml_env` is the name of the environment. You can use any name you prefer.

- `python=3.9` specifies the Python version. Python 3.9 is widely supported and compatible with most libraries.

Confirm the creation of the environment by typing "`y`" when prompted.

Step 4: Activate the environment

Activate the environment with:

```
conda activate qml_env
```
You'll notice that (`qml_env`) now appears at the beginning of your command prompt, indicating the environment is active.

Step 5: Install necessary libraries

Install the foundational libraries using the following commands:

```
conda install pandas numpy scikit-learn jupyter
```

If needed later, additional libraries can be installed using `pip`.

Step 6: Launch Jupyter Notebook

Jupyter Notebook, as we mentioned, is a user-friendly, interactive coding environment. Launch it by typing:

```
jupyter notebook
```
This command will open Jupyter Notebook in your default web browser. You can now create and manage notebooks for your Python projects.

Python's core libraries

With the environment set up, let's dive into the three critical libraries: pandas, NumPy, and scikit-learn. These tools will prepare you for handling data, performing numerical operations, and building machine learning models.

Manipulating Data from a CSV File

Pandas is the go-to library for handling datasets, particularly those stored in CSV (Comma-Separated Values) files. Let's assume you're working with a file named customer_data.csv, containing columns such as Customer_ID, Age, Income, and Defaulted; a typical example of a credit decision dataset.

Here's an example of how to load, explore, and manipulate this dataset:

```python
import pandas as pd

# Load the dataset from a CSV file
df = pd.read_csv('customer_data.csv')

# Display the first few rows of the dataset
print("First Few Rows of the Dataset:")
print(df.head())

# Summarize the dataset
print("\nSummary Statistics:")
print(df.describe())
```

This will be your output (using dummy data):

```
First Few Rows of the Dataset:
  Customer_ID  Age   Income  Defaulted
0 CST_000001   49   131993          0
1 CST_000002   43   115246          0
2 CST_000003   47   109268          1
3 CST_000004   60   133530          0
4 CST_000005   41   102622          1
```

```
Summary Statistics:
                Age           Income    Defaulted
count   1000.000000      1000.000000   1000.00000
mean      43.646000    105190.194000      0.50000
std        9.799015     22229.151176      0.50025
min       15.000000     39841.000000      0.00000
25%       37.000000     90960.750000      0.00000
50%       44.000000    103727.000000      0.50000
75%       50.000000    119564.500000      1.00000
max       75.000000    187495.000000      1.00000
```

Here the code begins by demonstrating how to load a dataset stored in a CSV file into a pandas DataFrame, a tabular data structure that provides powerful manipulation tools. The command `pd.read_csv('customer_data.csv')` reads the contents of the file `customer_data.csv` and stores it as a DataFrame object called `df`. This allows us to access and manipulate the dataset programmatically.

Next, the `df.head()` function is used to display the first few rows of the dataset, giving a quick glimpse of its structure, such as column names and a sample of the data. This is particularly useful for ensuring the file has been loaded correctly and understanding its layout.

To gain further insight into the dataset, the code uses `df.describe()`, which generates summary statistics for numerical columns. This provides metrics such as count, mean, standard deviation, minimum, and maximum values, helping us understand the overall distribution of the data.

NumPy: Performing Numerical Computations

NumPy is a high-performance library for numerical and array-based operations, essential for tasks involving matrices and linear algebra.

Here's how you can perform matrix multiplication using NumPy:

```python
import numpy as np

# Create two matrices
matrix_a = np.array([[1, 2], [3, 4]])
matrix_b = np.array([[5, 6], [7, 8]])

# Perform matrix multiplication
result = np.dot(matrix_a, matrix_b)

# Print the result
print(result)
```

And this would be your outcome:

```
[[19 22]
 [43 50]]
```

It begins with creating two matrices, `matrix_a` and `matrix_b`, using `np.array()`. Each matrix is defined as a 2x2 array of numbers. For example, `matrix_a` contains the values `[[1, 2], [3, 4]]`, and `matrix_b` contains `[[5, 6], [7, 8]]`. These matrices represent basic numerical data structures used in various mathematical and machine learning computations.

The next operation, `np.dot(matrix_a, matrix_b)`, performs matrix multiplication between the two matrices. Matrix multiplication is a fundamental operation in linear algebra and is commonly used in many machine learning algorithms, particularly in neural networks and data transformations. The result of the multiplication is stored in the variable `result`.

Scikit-learn: Building a Machine Learning Model with SVC

Scikit-learn provides simple yet powerful tools for building machine learning models. Here, we'll use the Support Vector Classifier (SVC), which is particularly effective for binary classification problems like predicting whether a customer defaults (e.g. failing to pay back a loan) or not.

```python
from sklearn.model_selection import train_test_split
from sklearn.svm import SVC
from sklearn.metrics import accuracy_score, roc_auc_score,
classification_report, confusion_matrix, roc_curve
import numpy as np
from sklearn.preprocessing import StandardScaler

# Assume 'df' is the DataFrame from the previous pandas
example

# Select features and the target variable
X = df[["Age", "Income"]]  # Features
y = df["Defaulted"]         # Target variable

# Split the dataset into training and testing sets
X_train, X_test, y_train, y_test = train_test_split(X, y,
test_size=0.20, random_state=42)

# Normalization
scaler = StandardScaler()
X_train = scaler.fit_transform(X_train)
X_test = scaler.transform(X_test)


# Train an SVC model
model = SVC(kernel='linear', probability=True)  #
probability=True to enable predict_proba
model.fit(X_train, y_train)

# Make predictions
y_pred = model.predict(X_test)
y_pred_proba = model.predict_proba(X_test)[:, 1]  # Get
probabilities for the positive class
```

```
# Calculate metrics
accuracy = accuracy_score(y_test, y_pred)
auc = roc_auc_score(y_test, y_pred_proba)

# Calculate KS statistic
fpr, tpr, thresholds = roc_curve(y_test, y_pred_proba)
ks = np.max(tpr - fpr)

# Classification report
class_report = classification_report(y_test, y_pred)

# Print the metrics
print(f"Accuracy: {accuracy:.4f}")
print(f"AUC: {auc:.4f}")
print(f"KS Statistic: {ks:.4f}")
print("Classification Report:\n", class_report)
```

Here is the outcome:

```
Accuracy: 0.5850
AUC: 0.6534
KS Statistic: 0.2652
Classification Report:
              precision    recall  f1-score   support

           0       0.57      0.53      0.55        96
           1       0.59      0.63      0.61       104

    accuracy                           0.58       200
   macro avg       0.58      0.58      0.58       200
weighted avg       0.58      0.58      0.58       200
```

This example showcases how to use scikit-learn to train and evaluate a machine learning model, specifically a Support Vector Classifier (SVC). The process begins by assuming the presence of a DataFrame df, created in the earlier pandas example, which contains columns like Age, Income, and Defaulted.

First, the dataset is prepared by selecting the features (Age and Income) and the target variable (Defaulted). These

---

are stored in the variables `X` (features) and `y` (target). The features represent the input data, while the target variable contains the labels the model is designed to predict.

Next, the data is split into training and testing sets using `train_test_split`. The training set (75% of the data by default) is used to fit the model, while the testing set (25% of the data) evaluates its performance. The `random_state=42` ensures that the split is reproducible, providing consistent results every time the code is executed. Also, we need to normalize the dataset to avoid different numerical scales affecting the performance of the model.

The SVC is then initialized with a linear kernel by calling `SVC(kernel='linear')`. The kernel determines how the model separates the data in the feature space. A linear kernel is suitable for datasets that are linearly separable. The `fit` method is used to train the model on the training data (`X_train` and `y_train`).

Once the model is trained, it makes predictions on the unseen test data using `model.predict(X_test)`. These predictions are stored in `y_pred`. On top of the previous, we extract probabilities to finally measure accuracy, AUC (Area Under the Curve), KS and the classification report.

QSVC using Qiskit

In this section, we'll implement a Quantum Support Vector Classifier (QSVC) using Qiskit, a powerful library for quantum computing. The QSVC uses quantum feature maps to encode classical data into a quantum state space, enabling better data separability for classification.

We'll begin by loading a dataset from a CSV file, preprocessing it with pandas, and applying Principal Component Analysis (PCA) to reduce its dimensionality while avoiding data leakage. Then, we'll use Qiskit's quantum feature maps and kernel methods to train a QSVC. Finally, we'll evaluate the QSVC's performance using key metrics such as accuracy, AUC, KS statistic, and a classification report as we did in the previous section.

To follow along, ensure that Qiskit and its machine learning extensions are installed. Activate your Python environment and run:

```
pip install qiskit-machine-learning matplotlib
```

Preparing the Dataset

The dataset, saved as `customer_data_plus.csv` now contains 20 features, as well as a target variable, `Defaulted` (indicating whether a customer has defaulted). Let's start by loading and inspecting this dataset using pandas.

```python
import pandas as pd

# Load the dataset from a CSV file
df = pd.read_csv('customer_data_plus.csv')

# Display the first few rows of the dataset
print("First Few Rows of the Dataset:")
print(df.head())

# Summarize the dataset
print("\nSummary Statistics:")
print(df.describe())

# Define X and y
```

```
X = df.drop(columns=["Customer_ID", "Defaulted"])    # Drop ID
and target
y = df["Defaulted"]  # Keep only the target variable
```

Here, the dataset is loaded into a pandas DataFrame and divided into X (features) and y (target). The head() method gives us a quick look at the dataset's structure.

PCA for Dimensionality Reduction

To prepare the data for a quantum feature map, we must reduce its dimensionality, as each feature requires additional qubits, which currently are a limited resource in quantum systems. Principal Component Analysis (PCA) is a dimensionality reduction technique that transforms high-dimensional data into a smaller number of dimensions while retaining the most significant patterns or variations in the dataset. It works by identifying the directions, called principal components, along which the data varies the most and projecting the data onto these components. By keeping only the top few principal components, PCA reduces the complexity of the data while preserving its essential variance, making it easier to visualize and process, especially for tasks like quantum encoding where fewer dimensions are needed to match the number of qubits.

```
from sklearn.decomposition import PCA
from sklearn.preprocessing import MinMaxScaler
from sklearn.model_selection import train_test_split

# Split the dataset into training and testing sets first
X_train, X_test, y_train, y_test = train_test_split(X, y,
test_size=0.20, random_state=42)

# Standardize features separately for training and testing
sets
scaler = MinMaxScaler()
X_train_scaled = scaler.fit_transform(X_train)
X_test_scaled = scaler.transform(X_test)
```

```
# Apply PCA only on the training data
pca = PCA(n_components=2)
X_train_pca = pca.fit_transform(X_train_scaled)

# Transform the test data using the PCA fitted on the training set
X_test_pca = pca.transform(X_test_scaled)
```

By splitting the data first, we ensure that the test set remains unseen during the dimensionality reduction to two components. PCA is fitted only on the training data (`X_train_sca led`) to learn its transformations, and these transformations are then applied to the test data (`X_test_scaled`) without leaking any information, thus replicating real-life production setups. Also, we applied a normalization process, but this time using a `MinMaxScaler` that will reduce the numerical range of all the features from 0 to 1.

Defining the Quantum Feature Map

A feature map in quantum computing is a method of encoding classical data into quantum states, allowing quantum algorithms to process and analyze the data. For this example, we use Qiskit's `ZZFeatureMap`, which specifically uses quantum gates to create entanglement between qubits and applies phase shifts based on the input data, effectively transforming it into a quantum representation. This process maximizes the separability of data points in the quantum state space, making it easier for quantum machine learning models to classify them. The entanglement introduced by the ZZFeatureMap leverages quantum mechanics to capture complex relationships in the data, which classical feature transformations struggle with.

```
from qiskit.circuit.library import ZZFeatureMap
from qiskit.visualization import circuit_drawer
```

```
# Define a 2-qubit feature map with more details
feature_map = ZZFeatureMap(feature_dimension=2, reps=2,
entanglement='linear')

# Decompose the feature map to show detailed gates
detailed_feature_map = feature_map.decompose()

# Draw the detailed feature map circuit
detailed_feature_map.draw(output='mpl')
```

This will be the circuit visualization:

The ZZFeatureMap initializes a 2-qubit feature map, matching the two dimensions of the PCA-transformed data. The reps=2 parameter increases the complexity of the feature map, while a linear entanglement scheme ensures that qubits interact effectively.

Training the QSVC

The FidelityStatevectorKernel in Qiskit computes the kernel matrix using the quantum feature map in a simulator (statevectors). This kernel is used to train the QSVC, which acts as a quantum-enhanced classifier.

```
from qiskit_machine_learning.kernels import
FidelityStatevectorKernel
from qiskit_machine_learning.algorithms.classifiers import
QSVC

# Define the quantum kernel using the feature map
quantum_kernel =
FidelityStatevectorKernel(feature_map=feature_map)

# Initialize and train the QSVC
model = QSVC(quantum_kernel=quantum_kernel, probability=True)
```

```
model.fit(X_train_pca, y_train)

# Make predictions
y_pred = model.predict(X_test_pca)
y_pred_proba = model.predict_proba(X_test_pca)[:, 1]  # Get
probabilities for the positive class
y_pred_proba = model.predict_proba(X_test)[:, 1]  # Get
probabilities for the positive class
```

When using a `FidelityStatevectorKernel`, the first step is to map each classical data point into a quantum state using a quantum feature map, such as the ZZFeatureMap. This feature map encodes the data into a quantum circuit by applying a series of gates, producing a unique quantum state for each data point. Once these states are prepared, the quantum kernel needs to measure how similar two data points are within this quantum representation.

To do this, the kernel uses the adjoint of the feature map, which is essentially the feature map run in reverse. Consider two data points, $x1$ and $x2$. The process starts by encoding $x1$ into a quantum state using the feature map. Next, instead of directly comparing this quantum state to $x2$, the adjoint of the feature map for $x2$ is applied to the state of $x1$. This operation aligns the quantum representation of $x2$ with $x1$, creating a setup where their similarity can be effectively measured. This step is important because it ensures the comparison is meaningful in the quantum space.

Once the adjoint feature map is applied, a measurement is performed on the resulting quantum state. This measurement reveals the overlap between the quantum states of $x1$ and $x2$, which is a number between 0 and 1. A value close to 1 means the data points are very similar in the quantum space, while a value close to 0 means they are very different.

The kernel computation doesn't stop with just one pair of data points. To fully understand the relationships within a dataset, this process is repeated for every pair of data points. The resulting similarity values are stored in a matrix called the kernel matrix, where each entry represents the similarity between two specific data points. This kernel matrix is then used by classical machine learning models, like Support Vector Machines, to identify patterns and make predictions.

By using the adjoint feature map, the kernel computation becomes symmetric and well-structured, capturing intrinsic patterns in the data. This symmetry and the quantum-enhanced representation make the quantum kernel particularly efficient in handling complex classification problems that classical approaches struggle to resolve.

Evaluating the QSVC

When evaluating the performance of a machine learning model, several metrics are used to understand how well the model is performing across several parameters. Each of these metrics tells a unique story about the model's ability to classify data accurately and make meaningful predictions.

```
from sklearn.metrics import accuracy_score, roc_auc_score,
classification_report, confusion_matrix, roc_curve
import numpy as np

# Calculate metrics
accuracy = accuracy_score(y_test, y_pred)
auc = roc_auc_score(y_test, y_pred_proba)

# Calculate KS statistic
fpr, tpr, thresholds = roc_curve(y_test, y_pred_proba)
ks = np.max(tpr - fpr)

# Classification report
class_report = classification_report(y_test, y_pred)
```

```
# Print the metrics
print(f"Accuracy: {accuracy:.4f}")
print(f"AUC: {auc:.4f}")
print(f"KS Statistic: {ks:.4f}")
print("Classification Report:\n", class_report)
```

Here is what you should obtain:

```
Accuracy: 0.9400
AUC: 0.9590
KS Statistic: 0.9000
Classification Report:
              precision    recall  f1-score   support

           0       0.92      0.96      0.94       100
           1       0.96      0.92      0.94       100

    accuracy                           0.94       200
   macro avg       0.94      0.94      0.94       200
weighted avg       0.94      0.94      0.94       200
```

The simplest and most understandable statistic is accuracy. It describes the model's capacity to produce correct forecasts, measured as the percentage of times the prediction was correct. For instance, if the accuracy is 85%, it means the model produced 85 accurate predictions out of 100. While accuracy is important, it may not provide a comprehensive view, especially when dealing with an imbalanced dataset where one class significantly outnumbers the other. In such situations, other metrics become absolutely essential to understand the actual performance of a model.

A more complex indicator of the model's capacity to separate between classes is the AUC, or Area Under the Curve. It plots the true positive rate—how frequently the model properly identifies a class—against the false positive rate—how often the model wrongly identifies a class—based on the ROC (Receiver Operating Characteristic) curve. AUC basically flattens this curve into one integer between 0 and 1. A flawless

---

model that can always differentiate between the classes would have an AUC of 1, whereas a model that is no better than randomly guessing would get an AUC of 0.5. When the dataset is skewed, this metric is particularly helpful, since it emphasizes the discriminative power of the model, instead of only raw, absolute correct responses (if a dataset has 99% of its records belonging to one class, a model that always predicts that same class will automatically achieve a 99% of accuracy, but would offer no information at all).

The biggest gap between the two classes' expected probabilities is measured by the KS (Kolmogorov-Smirnov) statistic. Simply put, it indicates, based on their probability distributions, how effectively the model can separate the positive from the negative class. Better separation—that is, the model does a good job assigning high probability to one class and low probability to the other—is indicated by a higher KS value. In risk analysis, especially in the financial sector where the capacity to separate classes is vital, this statistic is frequently employed.

The model's performance for every class in the dataset is thoroughly broken down in the classification report. It comprises several key metrics such as precision, which gauges the percentage of correct predictions among all predictions made for a given class. It also includes recall, which measures what percentage of all actual instances of a class were correctly identified by the model. The F1-score, which aggregates precision and recall into a single metric to balance their trade-offs, is also computed and presented in the report. Furthermore, included in the classification report are the total number of records for every class, providing a good overall picture of the general performance of the model.

These metrics, considered together and in contrast to each other, provide a comprehensive assessment of a model's performance, surpassing any of them separately, to provide a deeper understanding of how successfully the model performs, especially in real-world situations where data complexity and imbalances are frequent.

This application of a QSVC emphasizes the potential of quantum computing in machine learning processes. Starting with a CSV dataset, we separated and preprocessed the data, reduced dimensions and applied feature map encoding of the data into a quantum state space. After training and evaluation, the QSVC showed performance using measures like accuracy, AUC, KS statistic, and a classification report.

Other alternatives

The tools and models accessible to developers and researchers change with the evolution of quantum computing. Two prominent frameworks that stand out, together with Qiskit and PennyLane, are Cirq and Q#. Though they serve somewhat different purposes and audiences, both are meant to close the gap between theoretical quantum ideas and actual application. Let's investigate the special qualities of these models and their contribution to the field of quantum computers.

Focused on working with NISQ devices, Google created Cirq, a Python-based quantum computing platform. Cirq is meant to enable scientists and engineers to construct and replicate the quantum circuits that are best suited for these devices.

Cirq's basic focus is hardware awareness. This means it offers tools to build circuits considering the particular properties and constraints of the quantum hardware they will run on. To reduce the error rates of quantum processes, Cirq, for instance, makes it simple to manipulate qubit connectivity—how qubits are physically coupled on a device.

The simplicity and adaptability of Cirq fuel its power. Python programming allows you to build quantum circuits while the framework provides simple ways to run these circuits on a representation of real quantum processors, such as those provided by Google's quantum hardware.

Conversely, Microsoft developed a quantum-oriented programming language called Q# as part of their Azure Quantum platform. Q# is a separate language especially designed for quantum programming, unlike Python-based systems like Cirq and Qiskit. It's a fascinating tool for creating quantum algorithms since its syntax and structure reflect a natural expression of quantum ideas.

The focus of Q# on modularity and scalability is noteworthy. Quantum programs in Q# are designed as reusable components—that is, operations and functions—that can be combined to produce increasingly intricate algorithms. Q# is especially appealing for large-scale quantum software development since its modular approach fits very nicely with the principles of contemporary software engineering.

Q# also works relatively well with conventional programming environments such as Python and C#. This lets developers create hybrid quantum-classical systems in which a more familiar language handles the classical components while the quantum component of the algorithm is expressed in Q#. For researchers investigating several technologies, Azure Quantum allows Q# programs to be carried out on a range of quantum hardware platforms, therefore offering a flexible solution.

Although both Cirq and Q# are rather strong, the particular objectives of the user usually determine which of them is better suited to their needs. Researchers working on near-term quantum algorithms and hardware-aware optimizations will find Cirq's Python-based methodology and emphasis on NISQ devices to be quite appealing. Those already familiar with Python and wishing to explore circuits running on contemporary quantum computers will find it natural.

On the other hand, Q# is a specialized language meant for people who wish to delve deeper into quantum programming with a focus on scalability and modularity. For developers interested in hybrid quantum-classical processes and long-term quantum software projects, its connection with Microsoft's Azure Quantum ecosystem makes it an interesting option.

Further Reading

Machine Learning for Imbalanced Data:
    https://www.packtpub.com/en-us/product/machine-learning-for-imbalanced-data-9781801070836

Python Machine Learning:
    https://www.packtpub.com/en-ec/product/python-machine-learning-9781789955750

Quantum Feature Map:
    https://pennylane.ai/qml/glossary/quantum_feature_map

What are support vector machines (SVMs)?:
    https://www.ibm.com/think/topics/support-vector-machine

Robust performance metrics for imbalanced classification problems:

https://arxiv.org/abs/2404.07661

Introduction to the quantum programming language Q#:
https://learn.microsoft.com/en-us/azure/quantum/qsharp-
overview

CHAPTER 5

The Relevance of the Preprocessing Phase

Introduction

A fundamental stage in any quantum machine learning process is the classical preprocessing step, which fills in for the gap between the current restrictions of quantum hardware and the complexity of real-world data. Many quantum algorithms require one qubit per feature of the input data, so the number of qubits directly determines the dimensionality of the data that can be encoded. Real-world datasets, however, can have hundreds or even thousands of features—far more than the capacity of present quantum computers (or even simulators). Techniques for dimensionality reduction become crucial for condensing data into a reasonable dimension so that quantum systems may efficiently handle it while preserving the most important information. Two of the most often used and successful technologies for dimensionality reduction are Principal Component Analysis (PCA) and Linear Discriminant Analysis (LDA).

PCA (we already demonstrated its use in the previous chapter) is an unsupervised method that finds the directions, or components, in the data that best explain variance, hence lowering dimensionality. It finds its eigenvectors and eigenvalues by first computing the covariance matrix of the dataset to capture the interactions between features. Whereas the eigenvalues show the degree of this variance, the eigenvectors show the directions of maximal variance. Retaining the features explaining most of the variability of the dataset, PCA projects the data onto a lower-dimensional space defined by the eigenvectors with the biggest eigenvalues. By removing superfluous or less useful elements, this procedure guarantees the preservation of the most important trends in the data. PCA is especially helpful for quantum applications when preparing datasets for activities such as clustering, regression, or anomaly detection—where the objective is to comprehend broad patterns and structures without the requirement for class labels.

PCA:
component axes that maximize the variance

LDA:
maximizing the component axes for class-separation

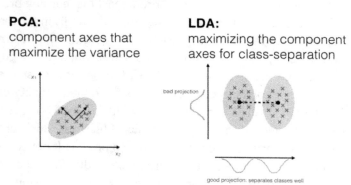

Figure 11: This figure compares PCA and LDA. PCA focuses on maximizing variance along principal component axes, while LDA optimizes axes for class separation, emphasizing projections that improve class distinguishability.
Source: https://sebastianraschka.com/Articles/2014_python_lda.html

By comparison, a supervised method meant to maximize class separability is LDA. Unlike PCA, which just considers variance, LDA considers data labels to improve its capacity to discriminate between various classes. LDA gets this done by computing the mean vectors of every class and evaluating how characteristics vary within a class (intraclass scatter) and how much the classes vary from one another (interclass scatter). LDA finds a projection maximizing the separation between classes by optimizing the ratio of interclass scatter to intraclass scatter. The data is then projected onto this lower-dimensional space such that the most pertinent traits for categorization are preserved. In quantum machine learning applications involving supervised learning, such as credit scoring or fraud detection, where the capacity to distinguish between classes is vital, LDA is extremely useful.

The dataset type and the overall objective of the resulting quantum model determine whether PCA or LDA is the optimal choice. PCA offers a general-purpose reduction of dimensionality by concentrating on variance, so it's more suitable when the task is unsupervised or when the dataset lacks class labels. Conversely, LDA is recommended for supervised jobs where optimizing class separability takes precedence. LDA can improve the capacity of the quantum feature map to encode class-specific information, hence improving the effectiveness of QSVMs or kernel-based learning for downstream classification tasks.

Sometimes distinct phases of data preparation can be addressed using PCA and LDA in concert. After first lowering the dimensionality of a high-dimensional dataset to a size fit for quantum systems using PCA, LDA can then hone the lowered features to highlight class separability. This mix allows you to maximize the balance between adapting the features to the particular needs of the work and catching broad trends.

Quantum feature maps—which translate classical data into quantum states for processing in the Hilbert space—have a direct dependence on dimensionality reduction. Since they scale with qubit count, quantum feature maps are naturally sensitive to the quality and complexity of the input data. Pre-processing guarantees that the quantum system can concentrate its computational resources on the most important data aspects by reducing the dataset to its most significant features. Without this stage, noisy or redundant characteristics can undermine the quantum algorithm's efficiency, therefore producing less than ideal outcomes.

Apart from ensuring fit with quantum hardware, preprocessing using PCA or LDA improves the interpretability of quantum outcomes. These methods simplify the analysis and validation of quantum algorithm's outputs by reducing the data into its fundamental elements. When working with quantum systems, which can easily become black-box processes, this becomes even more relevant, emphasizing the importance of guaranteeing the quality of the input data.

LDA plus K-means: a valuable combination

As mentioned above, in QML, preparing data effectively is a crucial step in ensuring the success of the algorithms applied later on. To address this, we'll use a combination of LDA and K-means clustering—an unsupervised learning algorithm that divides data into K clusters by minimizing the distance between data points and their assigned cluster centers (see Further Reading for more information on K-means). These techniques complement each other, with K-means grouping features into clusters for better representation and LDA reducing dimensions by maximizing class separability. Clustering is essential in this process because if LDA is applied to the entire dataset, it will only provide a single dimension for projection due to its supervised nature of optimizing for class separation. However, by clustering the data first, we gain the flexibility to choose how many dimensions we want—since LDA can then be applied within each cluster separately, allowing for multiple dimensions instead of just one. This implementation exemplifies how to prepare data for QML while maintaining control over dimensionality reduction.

To begin with, we need to import the necessary libraries for data manipulation, visualization, and machine learning. These libraries provide the tools for processing the dataset and applying clustering and dimensionality reduction techniques.

```
import numpy as np
import pandas as pd
import matplotlib.pyplot as plt
from sklearn.model_selection import train_test_split
from sklearn.preprocessing import MinMaxScaler
from sklearn.discriminant_analysis import
LinearDiscriminantAnalysis as LDA
from sklearn.cluster import KMeans
```

Here, numpy and pandas handle data manipulation, matplotlib is used for visualization, and sklearn provides clustering, scaling, and dimensionality reduction functionalities. These tools are foundational for implementing and analyzing the preprocessing pipeline.

The first step in working with any dataset is loading it into memory.

```
# Load dataset
df = pd.read_csv('yourdataset.csv')   # Replace with your
dataset file path
```

By sampling the dataset, we reduce its size to something manageable for this example while maintaining a representative subset of the data.

Once the data is loaded, we separate the features (independent variables) from the target variable (dependent variable). This division ensures we can analyze how features relate to the target class, a key step for effective preprocessing.

```
# Prepare the data
X = df.drop(['target'], axis="columns")  # Replace 'target'
with the name of the target column
y = df['target']
X_train, X_test, y_train, y_test = train_test_split(X, y,
test_size=0.20, random_state=42)
```

Here, X contains the feature columns, while y holds the target variable. The dataset is split into training and testing sets, with 80% used for training and 20% reserved for evaluation. This ensures that the testing data is unseen during preprocessing, maintaining a fair assessment of model performance.

To understand the relationship between features and the target variable, we calculate the correlation of each feature with the target. This helps identify which features are most informative for later applying the clustering.

```
# Calculate feature correlations with target
correlations = X_train.corrwith(y_train)
```

Using K-means clustering, we group features based on their correlation with the target variable. This unsupervised method organizes the features into clusters, enhancing the dimensionality reduction process.

```
# Clustering features using K-means
num_dimensions = 2  # Number of dimensions or clusters
correlations_reshaped = np.reshape(correlations.values, (-1,
1))
kmeans = KMeans(n_clusters=num_dimensions,
random_state=0).fit(correlations_reshaped)
clusters = kmeans.labels_

# Group features into clusters
groups = [np.where(clusters == i)[0] for i in
range(num_dimensions)]
```

Each feature is assigned to one of two clusters (num_dimensions=2), based on the similarity of its correlation with the target variable. This step simplifies the feature set, grouping related features together.

Within each cluster, we apply LDA to reduce dimensionality further.

```
# Apply LDA to each feature cluster
features_lda = np.empty((X_train.shape[0], num_dimensions))
features_lda_test = np.empty((X_test.shape[0],
num_dimensions))

for i, group in enumerate(groups):
    lda = LDA(n_components=1)
    features_lda[:, i] = lda.fit_transform(X_train.iloc[:,
group], y_train).ravel()
    features_lda_test[:, i] = lda.transform(X_test.iloc[:,
group]).ravel()
```

Each cluster is reduced to a single dimension, with the resulting components emphasizing the differences between classes. The training and testing datasets are transformed accordingly.

Normalization ensures the reduced features are scaled to a uniform range, making them more compatible with quantum feature maps.

```
# Normalize the new features for QML
minmax_scaler = MinMaxScaler().fit(features_lda)
X_train_qml = minmax_scaler.transform(features_lda)
X_test_qml = minmax_scaler.transform(features_lda_test)
```

This implementation integrates K-means clustering and LDA to prepare a dataset for quantum machine learning. This process involves grouping features based on their relationships to the target variable, reducing dimensionality within each group, and normalizing the data for compatibility with quantum systems. By preprocessing the data in this structured way, we ensure that quantum algorithms operate on high-quality inputs, optimizing their performance while staying within hardware constraints. This pipeline highlights the essential collaboration between classical preprocessing and quantum computation, creating a robust foundation for QML applications.

Other plausible techniques

Many more dimensionality reduction methods can be used to efficiently preprocess classical data beyond PCA and LDA.

Designed to evaluate high-dimensional datasets in a few dimensions, t-Distributed Stochastic Neighbor Embedding (t-SNE) is a nonlinear dimensionality reduction technique. It preserves the local structure of the data such that related data points in the original space stay close to each other in the resulting reduced space. Unlike PCA, which is linear and emphasizes global variance, t-SNE is particularly effective in capturing nonlinear correlations and clustering patterns inside the data. Although t-SNE is mostly used for visualization, it can also preprocess data for quantum systems by stressing inherent clusters or structures that might guide feature selection or later encoding into quantum feature maps.

t-SNE has restrictions, though. Particularly for big datasets, it's computationally costly. Furthermore, its outcomes are sensitive to hyperparameters. Although this method is useful for data exploration, it must be used carefully for downstream quantum operations.

A scalable and quick substitute for t-SNE is Uniform Manifold Approximation and Projection (UMAP), which lowers dimensionality while maintaining both global and local data structure. It generates a lower-dimensional representation by first optimizing a graph representation of the data, therefore capturing its topological structure in a high-dimensional space. For datasets with complicated, nonlinear relationships especially, UMAP is quite appropriate.

UMAP's scalability is one of its advantages; it allows UMAP to rapidly analyze more data than t-SNE. It's also a good option for preparing data for QML since it provides more consistent results when used with similar parameter values. UMAP can assist in finding significant feature subsets or guide dimensionality reduction in a way that maintains the integrity of quantum calculations by capturing both clustering patterns and the global layout of data.

Another alternative is autoencoders, where neural networks learn a compressed representation. These are based on two basic components: a decoder reconstructing the original data from this representation and an encoder mapping the input data to a lower-dimensional latent space. Autoencoders find a lower-dimensional representation that preserves the most important information by "teaching" the network to reduce the reconstruction error.

Autoencoders are more versatile for complicated datasets than PCA, which makes assumptions of linear relationships, since they can model nonlinear interactions. Quantum feature maps can employ the latent representation produced by the encoder as input, therefore retaining nonlinear patterns in the data and, thus, lowering dimensionality. Furthermore, some variants, such as denoising autoencoders, are able to eliminate noise from the data, therefore enhancing the quality of the given features for the quantum system.

Autoencoders' reliance on high computing capabilities during training and their need for hyperparameter adjustment represent their main challenges. They are, nevertheless, very useful when working with big and complicated datasets.

A statistical technique called Independent Component Analysis (ICA) breaks out a multivariate signal into additive, independent components. It aims to identify the unmixing matrix separating the observed data from mixtures of statistically independent source signals, assuming these components are mixtures. Unlike PCA, which emphasizes variance, ICA maximizes statistical independence across components. Therefore, it's perfect for revealing latent sources in the data.

ICA can be used in QML to preprocess data, but independent signals must be found before encoding into feature maps. Medical datasets or financial time-series data, for instance, often incorporate independent signals blended with observable aspects. ICA can minimize data dimensionality by separating these signals while maintaining the most useful features.

For huge datasets where conventional techniques like PCA or LDA may be computationally impossible, random projections are especially appealing. Although they do not focus on optimizing certain properties like variance or class separability, their simplicity and efficiency make them a good preprocessing step when computational resources are constrained and the emphasis is on rapid dimensionality reduction for quantum systems.

Although they are not a dimensionality reduction technique per se, feature selection approaches seek to find the most pertinent characteristics from the original dataset. Methods like statistical tests (e.g., chi-square) or Recursive Feature Elimination (RFE) can order features according to their relevance to the target variable. By eliminating pointless or redundant features, these techniques simplify the data prior to quantum encoding, lowering dimensionality.

When a dataset includes numerous useless elements that could compromise the performance of quantum computers, feature selection is especially useful. Focusing on the most informative aspects helps to simplify input for quantum feature maps, complementing techniques such as PCA or LDA.

In summary, while linear techniques like PCA and LDA are useful for dimensionality reduction, they may struggle to capture nonlinear relationships in the data. In such cases, more flexible nonlinear methods—such as t-SNE or UMAP—can be employed, though they often come with higher computational costs. Neural network-based approaches, like autoencoders, provide even more adaptable representations but require careful tuning and substantial computational resources to be effective.

In quantum machine learning, where every qubit often denotes a feature, the equilibrium between dimensionality reduction and information retention is crucial. Techniques that maintain the structure and relationships in the data while matching the limitations of the quantum hardware allow quantum feature maps to run efficiently, hence optimizing the performance of quantum algorithms. We create the foundation for effective quantum computation by choosing the suitable dimensionality reduction method, therefore guaranteeing that the data is both meaningful and controllable in the quantum domain.

Further Reading

What is principal component analysis (PCA)?:
https://www.ibm.com/think/topics/principal-component-analysis

Implementing linear discriminant analysis (LDA) in Python:
https://developer.ibm.com/tutorials/awb-implementing-linear-discriminant-analysis-python/

What is k-means clustering?:
https://www.ibm.com/think/topics/k-means-clustering

Stochastic Neighbor Embedding with Gaussian and Student-t Distributions: Tutorial and Survey:
https://arxiv.org/abs/2009.10301

UMAP: Uniform Manifold Approximation and Projection for Dimension Reduction:
https://umap-learn.readthedocs.io/en/latest/

An Introduction to Autoencoders:
https://arxiv.org/abs/2201.03898

Deep Kernel Principal Component Analysis for Multi-level Feature Learning:
https://arxiv.org/abs/2302.11220

Chapter Figures

Figure 11: Visual comparison between PCA and LDA
https://sebastianraschka.com/Articles/2014_python_lda.html

CHAPTER 6

From Classical Data to Quantum States

Introduction

One of the most transforming and difficult steps of QML is the embedding of classical data into quantum states. The success of any QML model depends on this fundamental mechanism, sometimes referred to as quantum data encoding or embedding. Quantum algorithms can access classical information—numerical, categorical, or even unstructured data—by encoding, therefore enabling the exploitation of quantum properties.

While data representation in classical systems is somewhat simple, quantum systems need careful embedding of data. Driven by linear algebra and probability amplitudes, quantum states are naturally complicated. Encoding classical data means converting it into quantum states such that their structure is preserved and quantum computation is made possible. The performance of the model as well as the viability of running the quantum algorithm within the limitations of current hardware depend on the efficiency of this translation.

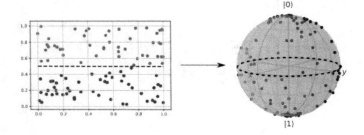

Figure 12: This figure shows a transformation of classical data points (left) into quantum states on the Bloch sphere (right). The mapping highlights how data is encoded into a quantum Hilbert space, with distinct regions for binary classification. The Bloch sphere depicts a single qubit representation of the data. Source: https://shafi-syed.medium.com/quantum-data-and-its-embeddings-1-3b022b2f1245

In this chapter, we'll investigate the most often used techniques for encoding classical data: basis encoding, angle encoding, and amplitude encoding. We'll also investigate the basis for kernel-based methods and other QML techniques—that of quantum feature maps, which translate data into high-dimensional quantum spaces. These methods affect model complexity, expressiveness, and generalization capacity by fundamentally changing the way data interact with quantum systems.

This technique is difficult, though. Significant obstacles are created by current hardware restrictions, noise, and circuit depth limits. Deciding the most suitable encoding method or feature map for a specific dataset and purpose is a non-trivial problem, often requiring many trials and fine-tuning. Using evolutionary algorithms and other optimization strategies, recent approaches have found the optimal feature map by balancing computing economy with predictive accuracy.

At last, we'll explore more general consequences of encoding on QML models. In what ways could the choice of encoding technique affect the generalizing capacity of a model? What trade-offs can we find between hardware limitations? And what paths do practitioners and researchers follow to overcome the present obstacles and release the complete possibilities of quantum data representations?

This chapter offers a thorough investigation of these subjects, equipping you with the necessary knowledge to decide which quantum encoding technique better suits your QML projects with wisdom. By the end, you will have a tight grasp of the ideas, techniques, and future directions guiding this important component of QML.

Encoding methods

To enable classical computers to process quantum data effectively, we require a method of translation. Quantum data encoding serves this purpose, transforming classical data into a quantum representation. Three fundamental techniques facilitate this transformation: basis encoding, amplitude encoding, and angle encoding (among others).

Basis encoding is the most direct approach, mapping classical bits (0s and 1s) to quantum states. It's akin to encoding a word by spelling out each letter, where each bit is assigned a corresponding qubit state. For instance, if a classical system represents the binary number 101, the quantum equivalent would be $|101\rangle$. This method is particularly advantageous for inherently binary datasets, such as those found in digital communication and text encoding.

Amplitude encoding leverages the amplitudes of quantum states to represent classical information, efficiently encoding large datasets into fewer qubits. A useful analogy is adjusting the intensity of multiple dimmer switches to represent different numerical values. For example, a set of real numbers such as 1.2,

2.7, 1.1, and 0.5 can be mapped into a quantum state by normalizing these values into probability amplitudes.

Angle encoding represents classical data by rotating qubits at specific angles, akin to positioning the hands of a clock to indicate different values. Each data point in a feature vector corresponds to a rotation, embedding information into quantum states. For example, a feature set $\{x1, x2, ..., xN\}$ can be transformed by rotating each qubit by an angle proportional to its respective value. This method can be effective for problems that naturally involve periodic functions or rotational symmetries.

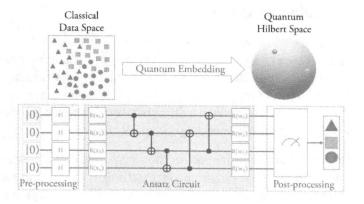

Figure 13: This figure illustrates quantum embeddings that map classical data into quantum Hilbert space, enabling inner products to represent relationships, similar to kernel methods. It also depicts a quantum machine learning model architecture, emphasizing the ansatz circuit's role in learning model weights based on input data. Source: https://ar-xiv.org/abs/2105.11853

Combined or hybrid encodings try to benefit from each technique's advantages. For large-scale applications, for instance, amplitude encoding might be utilized, while angle encoding works with localized data modifications. These methods provide more freedom so that researchers may balance the trade-off between the realistic hardware restrictions and the expressiveness of their quantum representations. Creative circuit design is common in hybrid approaches to interweave the several encoding techniques and guarantee that the resultant quantum state captures the pertinent features of the dataset. Although they show promise, these techniques introduce complexity and naturally require careful testing and validation.

The viability and efficiency of a QML method are strongly influenced by the chosen encoding technique. It determines the depth and complexity of the required quantum circuit, the expected error rate, and the capacity to scale to bigger datasets. Furthermore, it also affects the simplicity of interpreting and applying the quantum algorithm's outcomes in the next investigation (interpretability). Choosing the appropriate encoding affects the basic framework of the quantum computation and the insights it might offer.

Clearly, encoding is a basic component of the modeling process. As we delve further into the specifics of QML, it will become clear that it's far beyond a simple preparation stage. The effectiveness of the algorithm in finding patterns can be improved or hampered by the richness or sparsity of the data representation. Moreover, the limitations of modern quantum hardware sometimes call for innovative compromises. Encoding techniques are a hot topic of research with constant attempts to create useful but also efficient solutions for real-world problems.

Feature maps

During the encoding process, initial quantum states are prepared as a sequence of quantum gates maps the data into a richer, more expressive quantum feature space. In this space, relationships between data points—such as their similarity or separability—are captured in ways that classical techniques cannot reproduce. For example, quantum entanglement and interference patterns may reveal hidden structures in the data that remain inaccessible in lower-dimensional classical representations.

In the framework of kernel-based techniques—such as support vector machines—the idea of quantum feature maps is very powerful. In classical machine learning, kernels are mathematical functions that convert data into higher-dimensional spaces; therefore, enabling linear models to solve nonlinear problems. By using the unique characteristics of quantum systems to build kernels that capture even more complicated interactions, quantum feature maps expand this concept.

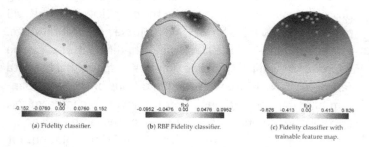

(a) Fidelity classifier.   (b) RBF Fidelity classifier.   (c) Fidelity classifier with trainable feature map.

Figure 14: This figure illustrates quantum classification methods: (a) a fidelity classifier, (b) an RBF fidelity classifier, and (c) a trainable feature map. The decision boundary (black line) separates two classes, with achieving ideal mapping by aligning class samples to opposite poles of the Bloch sphere in (c). Source: https://www.mdpi.com/1099-4300/25/6/860

Usually, a quantum feature map consists of a series of steps to use parameterized quantum circuits on the encoded data. Gates in these circuits are affected by the original data values, generating a new quantum state reflecting the changed interactions between data points. For instance, the feature map may have extra rotations and entangling gates to induce interactions between qubits, hence producing a richer representation of the data.

One example of a feature map is what we used in Chapter 4 for the QSVC approach. In that code we applied ZZ Feature Map which is designed to capture interactions between input features by leveraging entanglement. The ZZ name originates from the Ising-type interaction term $Z \otimes Z$ in quantum mechanics, where ZZ represents the Pauli-Z operator. The feature map encodes classical data into quantum states using a parameterized circuit that includes single-qubit rotations and controlled-Z (CZ) entangling gates. By applying these transformations, the ZZ feature map creates a quantum state that reflects correlations between input variables, enabling a richer and potentially more expressive representation than classical feature mappings. This makes it particularly useful for problems where feature interactions play a crucial role in classification or regression tasks.

The capacity of quantum feature maps to generate exponentially vast feature spaces with very few resources is among their most remarkable benefits. Just a few qubits can describe a feature space with dimensions way beyond its classical counterparts. This capacity allows us to address issues involving highly complicated or subtle patterns in the data, where traditional models struggle.

Quantum feature maps, however, also involve difficulties. Since the success of the method depends on the quality of data representation in the quantum space, the design of the feature map is absolutely critical. Inappropriate model performance results from poorly built feature maps, which either obscure relationships or add unnecessary complexity. Furthermore, the current quantum hardware also reduces feature maps' performance, since noise, limited qubit counts, and limited connections all affect the fidelity of the transformed states.

Researchers have started looking at automated and adaptive methods of creating quantum feature maps in order to overcome these difficulties. Variational quantum circuits, where the gate settings are optimized during training, for example, provide a means to customize the feature map to the particular dataset and task. Likewise, feature maps balancing expressiveness with practical limitations are being developed using evolutionary algorithms and other optimization methods.

The relationship between feature maps and encoding choice is also critical. While some encoding techniques, including amplitude encoding, easily fit some kinds of feature maps, others, like angle encoding, may need more complex adjustments to attain comparable degrees of expressiveness. Designing sensible QML models requires an awareness of these interconnections.

At last, the influence of quantum feature maps transcends single algorithms. They affect the scalability of the method, the interpretability of the model, and the possibility to get quantum advantage. Feature maps provide the means to fully realize quantum machine learning by turning data into a venue where quantum systems can shine.

Challenges of quantum encoding

Creating efficient quantum feature mappings and encodings requires both specialization and science, since you need to understand the trade-offs between hardware restrictions, expressiveness, and computational cost. Researchers are increasingly turning to genetic algorithms (GAs) as a powerful optimizer to navigate this complex terrain (discussed in detail in the next chapter). Motivated by the ideas of natural selection, GAs progressively change a population of candidate solutions—shown as quantum circuits or parameterized feature maps—toward an ideal configuration.

Within the framework of QML, evolutionary algorithms offer a methodical approach to investigate the large domain of feasible feature mappings and encodings. Every candidate in the population represents a particular arrangement of a quantum circuit, which can include decisions on the type of encoding (e.g. amplitude or angle), the gate sequence utilized in the feature map, and the gate parameter value. A fitness function guides the evaluation of these candidates by gauging their performance on a given job. On a classification task, the fitness function could represent the accuracy of a quantum kernel or the loss function of a variational quantum classifier.

Usually selected randomly or depending on past information, the process starts with producing an initial population of candidate feature maps. If the resources permit it, each candidate is then run on a quantum simulator or, in certain cases, real hardware. Every candidate's degree of fitness is computed, therefore offering a numerical assessment of their performance. This assessment identifies the top applicants who will kick start the following generation.

Two key procedures constitute the process of producing the next generation: crossover and mutation. Crossover preserves the beneficial features of the parents by combining aspects of two parent candidates to produce offspring, therefore promoting diversity. One parent might offer its encoding system, for instance, while the other supplies its series of entangling gates. Mutation brings little, random modifications to a candidate, including changing a gate parameter or adding a new circuit action. This randomness guarantees that the method can investigate a large spectrum of options, therefore avoiding local optima and raising the possibility of obtaining a global optimal solution.

As candidates with greater fitness are more likely to pass on their features, the population moves toward more effective feature maps and encodings after several consecutive generations. This iterative procedure lets genetic algorithms find new configurations that might not be obvious from a conventional optimization standpoint or by manual design.

Using genetic algorithms in QML has the additional benefit of incorporating the limitations of present quantum technology. To guarantee that the evolved feature maps are practical to implement on NISQ devices, the fitness function can include penalties for circuit depth or qubit use. In the same way, evolutionary algorithms can maximize feature maps for particular datasets or jobs, hence customizing their expressiveness to the current situation.

This procedure relies heavily on simulators, which offer a reasonably cheap approach to assess vast numbers of candidate feature maps. Running simulations allows researchers to evaluate a vast spectrum of setups without the effort and cost of using actual quantum hardware. Simulators can typically run circuits faster and with more dependability than physical devices. Thus, this method also enables quick iteration.

As a counterpoint, genetic algorithms face several challenges. Controlling the population size and the number of generations is crucial since the computational cost of assessing every candidate increases with the complexity of the quantum circuit. Furthermore, the choice of fitness function is a key factor; it has to be cheap enough to compute and fairly representative of the objectives of the QML work. Another important factor is finding the ideal balance between exploration and exploitation, thereby guaranteeing that the algorithm investigates several alternatives while concentrating on interesting directions.

These algorithms have been successfully applied to maximize feature maps for tasks including quantum kernel estimation, variational quantum classifiers, and quantum neural networks. With present quantum technology, they have shown the capacity to find innovative and efficient solutions, therefore stretching the bounds of what is feasible for this technology.

Further Reading

Quantum data encoding: a comparative analysis of classical-to-quantum mapping techniques and their impact on machine learning accuracy:
https://epjquantumtechnology.springeropen.com/articles/10.1140/epjqt/s40507-024-00285-3

Efficient quantum amplitude encoding of polynomial functions:
https://quantum-journal.org/papers/q-2024-03-21-1297/

Quantum Circuits, Feature Maps, and Expanded Pseudo-Entropy: A Categorical Theoretic Analysis of Encoding Real-World Data into a Quantum Computer:
    https://arxiv.org/html/2410.22084v1

How quantum and evolutionary algorithms can help each other: two examples:
    https://inspirehep.net/literature/2813849

Quantum Machine Learning: Exploring the Role of Data Encoding Techniques, Challenges, and Future Directions:
    https://www.mdpi.com/2227-7390/12/21/3318

Chapter Figures

Figure 12: Transformation of classical data into quantum states on the Bloch sphere
    https://shafi-syed.medium.com/quantum-data-and-its-embeddings-1-3b022b2f1245

Figure 13: Quantum embeddings and the role of ansatz quantum circuit in machine learning
    https://arxiv.org/abs/2105.11853

Figure 14: Quantum classification methods; Fidelity classifier, RBF fidelity, feature map
    https://www.mdpi.com/1099-4300/25/6/860

CHAPTER 7
Support Vector Classifiers

Introduction

Support Vector Machines (SVMs) are among the most solid and flexible methods for classification problems in the field of machine learning. Fundamentally, SVMs seek to create the best possible boundary—usually known as a decision boundary—between data points of several classes. Designed precisely to optimize the margin, or distance, between the nearest data points of every class, this boundary—known as a hyperplane—ensures a clear and dependable separation. SVMs shine in determining the ideal solution for linearly separable data, where the classes may be separated using a straight line (or a flat hyperplane in higher dimensions).

What happens then when the data is not linearly separable? Consider a dataset built of concentric circles where no straight line can divide the classes. Here is where kernels make the difference: they provide a data-transforming method for managing challenging datasets. Even if the data appears twisted or inseparable in its natural form, kernels allow SVMs to project data into a higher-dimensional space where it can be linearly separated. Mathematical shortcuts called kernel functions enable one to accomplish this clever trick without directly determining the coordinates of the data points in the higher-dimensional space.

Usually impractical for classical computers to compute or even depict, a quantum kernel maps data into an indefinitely huge feature space using a quantum computer. Data points indivisible in the classical world may become linearly separable in this quantum feature space, therefore allowing the SVM to create strong and unambiguous decision boundaries.

Quantum kernels are able to capture complex and subtle patterns in data by using the computational benefits of quantum systems. Quantum kernels have the ability to expose relationships between the data, which would otherwise remain concealed if only traditional kernels were to be applied. This capacity makes QSVMs, which combine the transforming power of quantum kernels with the classical ideas of SVMs, a fascinating tool for handling difficult classification issues.

We'll disentangle the mechanics of SVMs and kernels in this chapter, showing why they are fundamental for machine learning and how they operate for classification. After that, we'll enter the quantum domain and investigate the operations of quantum kernels as opposed to classical ones. We'll go over their useful applications, the difficulties you may face when using QSVMs, and their possibilities to transform machine learning down the road. Whether you have any prior knowledge of classical SVMs and quantum computing or not, this chapter seeks to provide a clear, thorough grasp of this transforming method.

The kernel trick

Let us first review the problem classical kernels are meant to solve so we can better appreciate their potential. Consider a basic two-dimensional dataset in which you must separate two groups of points—red and blue. A linearly separable dataset is defined by a group of points that can be accurately separated by a straight line; a conventional SVM can efficiently identify the appropriate line, or hyperplane, that divides the classes. What happens, though, when the dataset is not so straightforward? Examine the blue points encircling a little circle formed by the red points. No straight line—no matter how deftly placed—can split the two classes. Here is where kernels shine.

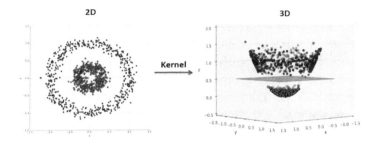

Figure 15: This figure shows a transformation of 2D data (left), where two classes are nonlinearly separable, into a 3D space (right) using a kernel. In 3D, the classes become linearly separable with a clear decision boundary (gray plane). Source: https://www.researchgate.net/publication/340610860_Multi-stage_Jamming_Attacks_Detection_using_Deep_Learning_Combined_with_Kernelized_Support_Vector_Machine_in_5G_Cloud_Radio_Access_Networks

By letting SVMs operate in higher-dimensional environments, where linear separation is feasible, kernels offer a mathematical solution to this problem. Kernels allow the SVM to map the data into a new space, sometimes referred to as the feature space, where the structure of the data may seem more linearly separable, instead of dealing with the data in its natural, non-separable form. Approaching datasets that are ordinarily inseparable in lower dimensions requires this switch to higher dimensions. But rather than explicitly computing the new coordinates for every data point in this feature space—a computationally costly process—kernels apply a mathematical shortcut. Known as the "kernel trick," this shortcut computes the associations, or similarities, between data points directly into the new space, without ever requiring the computation of the complete transformation.

The core of this procedure is the kernel function. It captures the way two data points relate to one another in the converted feature space, therefore measuring their similarity. A basic example of a kernel is the linear kernel, which computes the standard inner product of two data points. This is the simplest scenario whereby no change into a higher dimension is required. More complex kernels are applied to introduce nonlinear connections for non-linearly separable data. By raising the inner product of two data points to a power, the polynomial kernel, for example, adds curvature to the feature space, therefore faithfully capturing more complicated patterns. Often called the Gaussian kernel, the radial basis function (RBF) kernel is a potent tool for mapping data into an infinite-dimensional space and quantifying data point similarity based on distance. In the resulting space, the closer two points are, the more similar they are regarded for computation purposes. The sigmoid kernel is another example, which brings nonlinear changes, similar to the activation functions usually employed in neural networks.

The SVM never exactly computes the coordinates of the data in the higher-dimensional feature space when applying the kernel technique. Rather, it simply relies on the calculated similarity values obtained by the kernel function. This lets the SVM perform challenging classification tasks while avoiding the enormous computational cost of working in high-dimensional areas. Take the earlier scenario of a circular dataset, for instance. Although it's inseparable in its two-dimensional form, a basic transformation into three dimensions—by adding a new feature, such as the distance of each point from the center (or centroid)—can make it linearly separable. The SVM can sketch a flat hyperplane to divide the classes in this new three-dimensional space. The hyperplane corresponds to a nonlinear boundary, such as a circle, when this separation is reverted to the original two dimensions.

The essence of classical kernels is this capacity to convert nonlinear interactions into linear ones. From risk assessment to disease diagnosis, it allows SVMs to outperform other methods throughout a wide spectrum of classification challenges. Still, the success of this method mostly relies on the kernel and its parameters' choice. Choosing a kernel that fits the fundamental patterns in the data is absolutely vital. A bad choice might result in overfitting—where the model becomes overly suited to the training data and learns noise features, therefore, performing badly on unseen data—or underfitting—where the model fails to grasp the complexity of the data.

Classical kernels have restrictions even if the parameters are correctly set. Evaluating the kernel function can become impossible in very high-dimensional datasets or complex patterns, given their computational cost. Furthermore, some relationships in the data could be so complicated that even advanced kernels such as the RBF kernel cannot efficiently capture them. These constraints, however, could not apply to quantum kernels, which, using the ideas of quantum mechanics, can transform this process and get around the limitations.

Let's investigate how quantum kernels use the special features of quantum systems to overcome the difficulties experienced by conventional methods, therefore generating new opportunities for addressing challenging classification tasks.

The quantum kernel

In terms of how data may be converted and examined for machine learning applications, quantum kernels represent a significant advancement. Constructed on top of the ideas behind quantum mechanics, they expand the concept of classical kernels by projecting data into exponentially vast feature spaces using the special characteristics of quantum systems. Not only are these feature spaces computationally costly, but traditional approaches to represent them are often impossible. Particularly in cases of nonlinearly separable data, this capacity gives quantum kernels an edge in addressing challenging classification issues.

Reviewing the function of feature spaces will allow us to grasp how quantum kernels operate. Classical kernels transfer data into higher dimensions—where it becomes linearly separable—by means of mathematical adjustments. But the computational resources of classical systems essentially restrict the feature spaces that can be applied by classical approaches. Conversely, quantum kernels convert data into quantum feature spaces—spaces exponentially larger than their classical counterparts—by means of quantum circuits. Data point associations can be expressed in a far richer and more expressive way in this quantum feature space.

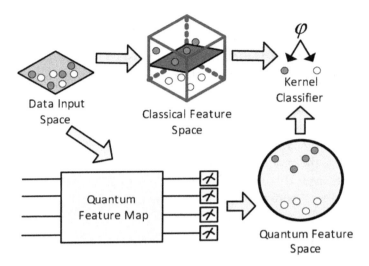

Figure 16: This figure illustrates the progression of data from the input space to feature spaces for classification. Classical feature space maps data using standard transformations, while the quantum feature map encodes data into a quantum space, enabling a kernel classifier to separate classes more effectively in higher-dimensional quantum Hilbert space. Source: https://www.researchgate.net/publication/373122191_Quantum-Enhanced_Support_Vector_Machine_for_Sentiment_Classification/figures?lo=1

The procedure starts with the preprocessing step, that is, encoding classical data into quantum states (a stage we have already covered at length in previous chapters). Quantum circuits work as the "kernel function", converting these quantum states into a new representation, highlighting the relationships and patterns in the data once they have been stored. The quantum circuit is carefully crafted to incorporate elements like entanglement, which generates qubit correlations, and interference, which either amplifies or suppresses particular probabilities. These quantum features allow the kernel to detect complicated, nonlinear relationships in the data, unreachable by means of classical approaches.

The quantum kernel function computes the similarity between two data points in the quantum feature space. This is done by measuring the overlap, or fidelity, between their corresponding quantum states. If the states exhibit high similarity, their overlap will be substantial; conversely, if they are dissimilar, the overlap will be small. Just as in a classical setting, the SVM then constructs the decision boundary in the quantum feature space using this similarity measure. However, because the quantum feature space is much larger and more expressive, the decision boundary can capture complex patterns more effectively, enabling the model to categorize data with greater sophistication.

The potential of quantum kernels to offer exponential scalability in feature space without requiring exponential computational resources puts them among the most fascinating features. A quantum system with a few dozen qubits, for example, can depict feature spaces with dimensions well beyond the grasp of conventional approaches. When studying high-dimensional data—such as genetic data, financial time series, or quantum chemistry datasets—where the complexity of the interactions typically exceeds the capability of conventional algorithms—this scaling creates new opportunities.

Quantum kernels come with difficulties, though. Using them requires quantum hardware, which is still in its early phases of development. In quantum systems, noise and decoherence can introduce errors into the kernel calculation, therefore influencing the accuracy of the produced model. At the same time, as mentioned above, using simulators still requires a large amount of classical resources, while quantum kernels on simulators are significantly slower than classical ones. Furthermore, the design of the quantum circuit applied for the kernel operation is crucial and non-trivial. On NISQ systems, the circuit must be shallow enough to be practical yet expressive enough to capture the complexity of the data. Establishing efficient quantum kernels depends mostly on optimizing this trade-off.

Another pragmatic difficulty is that quantum kernels might not always outperform classical kernels; it depends on the specific dataset or job. Their benefit comes from their capacity to find trends unattainable with traditional approaches. Because of their maturity and reduced processing burden, classical kernels may nevertheless perform just as well—if not better—for rather simple datasets or tasks. Consequently, the specific characteristics of each dataset or problem must drive the decision on the quantum kernel to be used.

Notwithstanding these difficulties, quantum kernels' potential is enormous. They are already showing value in multiple use cases. Quantum kernels provide a route to solve long-considered insurmountable challenges for conventional machine learning techniques, by using the "special powers" of quantum systems.

Simulating using all the cores

Due to its computational complexity, simulating quantum kernels on conventional hardware is one of the main difficulties in quantum machine learning. Computing a quantum kernel matrix for datasets with N samples means assessing N^2 quantum circuits (see Chapter 4 for the definition of a kernel matrix). Particularly with high-fidelity feature maps, every circuit simulation requires large computational resources. Large datasets make this quadratic scaling impracticable since it soon becomes a bottleneck as the dataset size increases.

By spreading the task over several CPU cores and thereby substantially lowering execution times, parallelism can help to reduce this problem. Here we present the Python module joblib, which offers a simple solution for parallelizing computing chores. Joblib allows us to compute quantum kernel matrices far quicker without sacrificing accuracy. Showing the notable speed increases obtained with joblib, this version defines the quantum kernel using PennyLane and shows both sequential and parallel ways for kernel computing.

In the following paragraphs, we'll describe how a QSVC approach can be implemented using PennyLane (previously we used Qiskit) and take advantage of using all the CPU cores to reduce the wall time of the execution.

We begin by creating a synthetic dataset using scikit-learn. The dataset includes features that will be encoded into quantum states.

```python
import numpy as np
from sklearn.datasets import make_classification
from sklearn.model_selection import train_test_split

# Create a synthetic dataset

X, y = make_classification(n_samples=200, n_features=4,
n_informative=2, n_redundant=0, n_classes=2, random_state=42)

# Split into training and testing datasets

X_train, X_test, y_train, y_test = train_test_split(X, y,
test_size=0.2, random_state=42)
```

This step generates a dataset with 200 samples and 4 features, simulating a binary classification problem. The data is split into 80% training and 20% testing subsets for model evaluation.

The quantum kernel encodes classical data into quantum states using a feature map and then measures the fidelity between pairs of encoded states.

```
import pennylane as qml

# Setup the quantum device and number of qubits

n_qubits = X_train.shape[1]
dev = qml.device("default.qubit", wires=n_qubits, shots=None)

# Define the quantum feature map using angle encoding

def feature_map(x):
    for i, val in enumerate(x):
        qml.RX(val, wires=i)

# Define the quantum kernel circuit

@qml.qnode(dev)
def kernel_circuit(x1, x2):
    feature_map(x1)
    qml.adjoint(feature_map)(x2)
    return qml.expval(qml.Projector([0] * n_qubits,
wires=range(n_qubits)))
```

The feature map encodes each feature of the classical data as a rotation around the X-axis for a specific qubit. The kernel circuit measures the overlap (fidelity) between two quantum states, representing the similarity of their corresponding classical data points.

The kernel matrix (see Chapter 4 for the definition of the kernel matrix) is computed row by row by iterating over all pairs of training samples. This approach does not use parallelization.

```
def compute_kernel_row(i, X1, X2):
    return [kernel_circuit(X1[i], X2[j]) for j in
range(X2.shape[0])]

def quantum_kernel_serial(X1, X2):
    m1 = X1.shape[0]
```

```
K = np.zeros((m1, X2.shape[0]))
for i in range(m1):
    K[i, :] = compute_kernel_row(i, X1, X2)
return K
```

This method loops through all rows and columns of the kernel matrix, computing the fidelity for each pair of data points. While this solution is correct, it quickly becomes inefficient as the dataset size increases, as the complexity scales quadratically with the number of samples. To speed up the computation, we use joblib to distribute the workload across multiple CPU cores.

```
from joblib import Parallel, delayed

def quantum_kernel_parallel(X1, X2, n_jobs=-1):
    m1 = X1.shape[0]
    rows = Parallel(n_jobs=n_jobs, verbose=10)(
        delayed(compute_kernel_row)(i, X1, X2) for i in
range(m1)
    )
    return np.array(rows)
```

Here, each row of the kernel matrix is computed in parallel by different workers. The n_jobs=-1 argument ensures that all available CPU cores are used and verbose=10 provides progress updates during execution. To quantify the performance improvement, we compare the execution times of the sequential and parallel implementations.

```
import time

# Compute kernel matrix serially

start_time = time.time()
K_train_serial = quantum_kernel_serial(X_train, X_train)
K_test_serial = quantum_kernel_serial(X_test, X_train)
no_parallel_time = time.time() - start_time
```

```
# Compute kernel matrix in parallel

start_time = time.time()
K_train_parallel = quantum_kernel_parallel(X_train, X_train,
n_jobs=-1)
K_test_parallel = quantum_kernel_parallel(X_test, X_train,
n_jobs=-1)
parallel_time = time.time() - start_time

# Print results

print("=== Comparison of Precomputation Times ===")
print(f"No parallelization: {no_parallel_time:.4f} seconds")
print(f"Parallelization    : {parallel_time:.4f} seconds\n")
```

This section measures and compares the time taken to compute the kernel matrices using the sequential and parallel methods. Typically, the parallel approach is significantly faster, especially for larger datasets. The speedup achieved by parallelization can be substantial, often reducing the execution time by orders of magnitude.

Finally, we validate that the serial and parallel methods produce identical kernel matrices and use the precomputed kernel to train an SVM.

```
from sklearn.svm import SVC

# Validate kernel matrices

assert np.allclose(K_train_serial, K_train_parallel, atol=1e-6)
assert np.allclose(K_test_serial, K_test_parallel, atol=1e-6)

# Train SVM using the parallel-computed kernel

qsvc = SVC(kernel='precomputed')
qsvc.fit(K_train_parallel, y_train)
accuracy = qsvc.score(K_test_parallel, y_test)

# Print accuracy

print(f"SVM Accuracy: {accuracy:.4f}")
```

We ensure that both methods produce equivalent kernel matrices by checking their numerical closeness. The SVM is then trained using the parallel-computed kernel, confirming that the parallelization does not compromise accuracy.

For a dataset with 200 samples and a 4-qubit feature map, the sequential computation of the kernel matrix took approximately 35.9 seconds, while the parallelized version completed in just 8.4 seconds—more than 4x improvement in performance (the absolute execution times are PC specs-dependent; however, the 4x improvement was the same in different PCs tested). This demonstrates the impact that parallelization can have when scaling quantum kernel computations on classical hardware, making it a practical option for larger datasets.

Multiple kernel learning

The goal of a multiple kernel learning approach is to combine different quantum kernels generated from separate encoding methods—amplitude encoding and angle encoding—into a single kernel matrix that maximizes the alignment with the target labels (in this particular case). This combined kernel is then used to train a QSVM, leveraging the diversity of encoding strategies for better classification performance. Let's break this down step by step.

In this example, we assume that dimensionality reduction and normalization techniques have already been applied, resulting in a dataset with a handful of features available to be simulated. It's also important to import all the necessary libraries.

The quantum device when using Pennylane is initialized using `qml.device`, which simulates a quantum computer.

Two encoding methods are defined: amplitude encoding and angle encoding.

```
import pennylane as qml

# Quantum device and encoding functions

dev = qml.device("lightning.qubit", wires=n_qubits)

def amplitude_encoding(x):
    return qml.AmplitudeEmbedding(x, wires=range(n_qubits),
normalize=True, pad_with=0.)

def angle_encoding(x):
    return qml.AngleEmbedding(x, wires=range(n_qubits))

@qml.qnode(dev)
def kernel_circuit1(x):
    amplitude_encoding(x)
    return qml.state()

@qml.qnode(dev)
def kernel_circuit2(x):
    angle_encoding(x)
    return qml.state()
```

Amplitude encoding maps the input vector into the amplitudes of a quantum state, ensuring efficient use of the Hilbert space for high-dimensional data. Angle encoding, on the other hand, maps data to quantum states by rotating qubits around specific axes, such as the X-axis. Each encoding captures different aspects of the data, and their combination can create a richer representation as we mentioned in Chapter 6.

The two quantum circuits, `kernel_circuit1` and `kernel_circuit2`, apply these encodings to the input data and return the resulting quantum states.

For efficiency, the quantum circuits are executed for each data point to precompute the resulting quantum states. This step avoids repeated execution of quantum circuits during the kernel matrix computation.

```
# Precompute quantum circuit outputs

def precompute_quantum_outputs(X, kernel_circuit):
    return np.array([kernel_circuit(x) for x in X])

# Precompute circuit outputs

X_train_circuit1 = precompute_quantum_outputs(X_train,
kernel_circuit1)
X_test_circuit1 = precompute_quantum_outputs(X_test,
kernel_circuit1)
X_train_circuit2 = precompute_quantum_outputs(X_train,
kernel_circuit2)
X_test_circuit2 = precompute_quantum_outputs(X_test,
kernel_circuit2)
```

Here, the training and test datasets are transformed using both encoding methods, producing quantum states that are stored for subsequent kernel matrix computations. Precomputing these outputs significantly reduces computational overload when dealing with large datasets.

The kernel matrix measures the similarity between data points based on their encoded quantum states. The similarity is computed as the squared magnitude of the inner product (fidelity) between two quantum states.

```
# Define number of CPU cores to be used (in this case, all of
them are being used "-1")

n_jobs=-1

# Compute kernel matrix using precomputed outputs with
parallelization
```

```
def compute_kernel_matrix_parallel(precomputed_X1,
precomputed_X2, n_jobs=n_jobs):
    """
    Computes the kernel matrix in parallel using joblib.
    """
    n_samples_1 = precomputed_X1.shape[0]
    n_samples_2 = precomputed_X2.shape[0]

    def kernel_value(i, j):
        # Compute the kernel value (similarity) for a pair of
quantum states
        return np.abs(np.dot(precomputed_X1[i],
precomputed_X2[j].conj())) ** 2

    # Generate all (i, j) index pairs to compute the kernel
matrix
    pairs = [(i, j) for i in range(n_samples_1) for j in
range(n_samples_2)]

    # Compute kernel values in parallel
    kernel_values = Parallel(n_jobs=n_jobs)(
        delayed(kernel_value)(i, j) for i, j in pairs
    )

    # Fill the kernel matrix
    kernel_matrix = np.zeros((n_samples_1, n_samples_2))
    for (i, j), value in zip(pairs, kernel_values):
        kernel_matrix[i, j] = value

    return kernel_matrix

# Compute kernel matrices
kernel_matrix1 =
compute_kernel_matrix_parallel(X_train_circuit1,
X_train_circuit1, n_jobs=n_jobs)
kernel_matrix2 =
compute_kernel_matrix_parallel(X_train_circuit2,
X_train_circuit2, n_jobs=n_jobs)

test_kernel_matrix1 =
compute_kernel_matrix_parallel(X_test_circuit1,
X_train_circuit1, n_jobs=n_jobs)
```

```
test_kernel_matrix2 =
compute_kernel_matrix_parallel(X_test_circuit2,
X_train_circuit2, n_jobs=n_jobs)
```

This function uses `joblib` for parallelization, distributing the computation of each kernel value across multiple CPU cores (in this case, the parameter of `n_jobs` is defined as -1 to use all the cores). This approach, as we mentioned previously, speeds up the process, especially for large datasets.

Kernel matrices are computed for both training and test datasets using the outputs of `kernel_circuit1` and `kernel_circuit2`.

The following step combines the kernel matrices from different encodings to create a final kernel matrix that best aligns with the target labels. This alignment is optimized through a convex optimization function, ensuring that the combined kernel represents the relationships in the data.

```
# Multiple Kernel Learning with Alignment

def compute_target_kernel(y):
    """
    Computes the target kernel matrix based on the labels.
    Each entry is the product of the labels for two data
points.
    """
    labels = y.to_numpy().reshape(-1, 1)
    return labels @ labels.T

def optimize_kernel_weights(kernel_matrices, target_kernel):
    """
    Optimizes the weights for combining kernel matrices to
maximize alignment with the target kernel.
    """
    n_kernels = len(kernel_matrices)

    # Define optimization variable for weights
```

```
    weights = cp.Variable(n_kernels, nonneg=True)  # Non-
negative weights

    # Compute the combined kernel matrix as a weighted sum
    combined_kernel = sum(weights[i] * kernel_matrices[i] for
i in range(n_kernels))

    # Define the alignment objective
    # Alignment = <K_combined, K_target> / (||K_combined||_F *
||K_target||_F)
    numerator = cp.trace(combined_kernel @ target_kernel)
    denominator = cp.norm(combined_kernel, "fro") *
cp.norm(target_kernel, "fro")

    # Define the optimization problem: maximize alignment
    objective = cp.Maximize(cp.trace(combined_kernel @
target_kernel))
    constraints = [cp.sum(weights) == 1]  # Weights must sum
to 1
    problem = cp.Problem(objective, constraints)

    # Solve the optimization problem using DQCP mode
    problem.solve(qcp=True, solver=cp.SCS, max_iters=500000,
eps=1e-6, verbose=True)

    # Return the optimized weights
    return weights.value
```

The target for kernel alignment is defined by creating a matrix that represents the relationships between the labels of the training data points. This matrix, called the target kernel, captures how similar or dissimilar each pair of data points is based on their class labels. If two points belong to the same class, their corresponding entry in the matrix is positive, representing similarity. Conversely, if the points belong to different classes, the entry is negative, indicating dissimilarity. The target kernel acts as a benchmark for combining multiple kernel matrices, ensuring that the final combined kernel closely aligns with the structure and relationships in the training data. This alignment helps the model understand the data's class distribution more effectively, leading to improved classification performance. The optimization aligns the combined kernel with this target by solving for non-negative weights that maximize the alignment. The optimized weights are then used to combine the kernel matrices. For the optimization we use Disciplined Quasiconvex Programming (DQCP) which refers to a mode in the convex optimization library CVXPY, that allows solving quasiconvex optimization problems. Unlike strictly convex or linear programs, quasiconvex problems involve objective functions that may not be convex but still exhibit properties that enable efficient optimization.

```
# Compute the target kernel matrix

target_kernel = compute_target_kernel(y_train)

# Optimize the weights for the kernel matrices

kernel_matrices = [kernel_matrix1, kernel_matrix2]
optimized_weights = optimize_kernel_weights(kernel_matrices,
target_kernel)

# Combine the kernel matrices using the optimized weights

final_kernel_matrix = sum(w * K for w, K in
zip(optimized_weights, kernel_matrices))
test_combined_kernel_matrix = sum(
    w * K_test for w, K_test in zip(optimized_weights,
[test_kernel_matrix1, test_kernel_matrix2])
)
```

The final combined kernel matrix is used to train a QSVM. The model is evaluated on the test set using the AUC metric.

```
# Train and evaluate the model

svc = SVC(kernel="precomputed", probability=True,
class_weight="balanced")
svc.fit(final_kernel_matrix, y_train)

# Predict on the test data and return the probabilities for
each class
```

```
predictions_qsvc =
svc.predict_proba(test_combined_kernel_matrix)[:, 1]

# Evaluate the model using AUC

auc_test = roc_auc_score(y_test, predictions_qsvc)
print("AUC for the test set (MKL-QSVC):", auc_test)
```

By combining the kernel matrices, the QSVM leverages the strengths of both encoding methods, achieving better classification performance. This multiple kernel learning approach demonstrates the flexibility of the quantum kernel framework and its ability to adapt to diverse data representations.

The final combined kernel matrix is visualized to provide insights of the structure of the data in the quantum feature space.

```
# Visualization of the kernel matrix

def plot_kernel_matrix(kernel_matrix, title):
    plt.imshow(kernel_matrix, cmap='hot',
interpolation='nearest')
    plt.colorbar()
    plt.title(title)
    plt.show()

plot_kernel_matrix(final_kernel_matrix, "Final Combined
Kernel")
```

The heatmap illustrates the similarities between data points, allowing us to interpret the identified relationships.

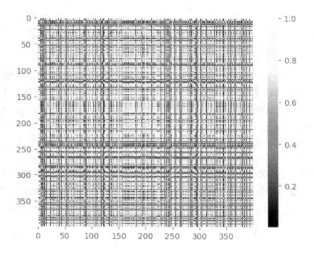

Figure 17: Plotted heatmap illustrating the similarities between the dummies data points of the yourdataset.csv dataset.

Amplitude encoding and angle encoding, for example, emphasize different aspects of the input data, and their combination creates a richer representation. By optimizing the weights when combining these kernels, the approach maximizes the final kernel matrix's correlation with the target labels, leading to improved classification performance.

Moreover, this framework is extensible. This flexibility enables the exploration of richer feature spaces, enhancing the model's ability to separate complex data distributions. As quantum hardware advances, these methods will become even more powerful, making MKL an eventual cornerstone of QML.

Genetic algorithms for the right feature map

Genetic algorithms are optimization techniques inspired by natural selection. They work by evolving a population of candidate solutions through iterative steps of mutation, crossover, and selection. This approach is particularly effective for exploring large, complex solution spaces where traditional optimization methods might struggle.

In QML, genetic algorithms offer a way to automatically design and optimize quantum feature maps—critical components of QSVMs. As already mentioned, a feature map determines how classical data is encoded into quantum states, directly impacting the effectiveness of the quantum kernel in separating data classes. Designing these feature maps manually is challenging, as it involves balancing expressiveness, computational efficiency, and hardware constraints. Genetic algorithms automate this design process, finding optimal feature maps that improve accuracy while keeping circuit complexity manageable.

A method proposed by Sergio Altares-López, Angela Ribeiro, and Juan José Garćıa-Ripoll uses a multiobjective genetic algorithm (NSGA-II) to optimize both the structure and parameterization of quantum feature maps for QSVMs. Their approach prioritizes accuracy and generalization while minimizing circuit size, resulting in interpretable, low-entanglement feature maps suitable for hybrid quantum-classical strategies. Below, we'll implement this technique step-by-step using Python code.

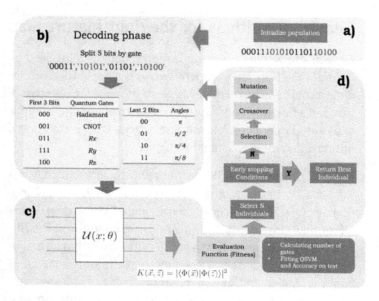

Figure 18: Technique scheme: (a) Initialize the population. (b) Decode using five bits per quantum gate and angle. (c) Evaluate fitness with QSVM based on accuracy and gate count. (d) Repeat genetic algorithm until early stopping, yielding the optimized ansatz. Source: https://iopscience.iop.org/article/10.1088/2058-9565/ac1ab1

Before implementing the genetic algorithm, it's necessary to set up the environment by importing the necessary libraries and custom modules. Ensure the repository referenced in the paper is downloaded, as it contains essential components for circuit design, fitness evaluation, and genetic optimization: https://github.com/sergio94al/Automatic_design_of_quant um_feature_maps_Genetic_Auto-Generation. It's relevant to remember that the correct version of Qiskit and Python is needed for this to work, since newer versions might not work with these methods due to deprecated functions within the libraries.

```
# Import necessary libraries and custom modules

import numpy as np
import pandas as pd
import matplotlib.pyplot as plt
import importlib

# Load custom modules for genetic algorithms and QSVMs
(relevant to use the GitHub repo associated)

import circuit
import encoding
import qsvm
import fitness
import gsvm
importlib.reload(circuit)
importlib.reload(encoding)
importlib.reload(qsvm)
importlib.reload(fitness)
importlib.reload(gsvm)

import time
```

These modules handle various tasks, including defining quantum circuits (`circuit`), evaluating their fitness (`fitness`), and implementing the genetic algorithm (`gsvm`).

The genetic algorithm evolves a population of candidate circuits to find optimal feature maps. It uses a multiobjective approach, balancing classification performance and circuit complexity (sometimes referred to as the parsimony principle).

```
# Define the genetic algorithm function

def evol(output="sample_result.csv"):
    y = y_train   # Training labels
    X = X_train   # Training features

    # Start the timer to measure performance
    start = time.time()

    # Run the genetic algorithm with specified parameters
```

```
    pop, pareto, logbook = gsvm.gsvm(
        nqubits=2,              # Number of qubits
        depth=4,                # Circuit depth
        nparameters=2,          # Number of tunable parameters
        X=X, y=y,               # Training data and labels
        weights=[-1.0, 1.0],    # Weighting accuracy and circuit
complexity
        mu=50,                  # Population size
        lambda_=10,             # Number of offspring
        ngen=150                # Number of generations
    )

    # Print the time taken for the genetic algorithm to finish

    print(f'Simulation finished after {time.time() - start}
seconds')

    # Save the Pareto-optimal solutions to a CSV file

    print(f'\nGenetic-algorithm output ({output})')
    print('---------------------------------')
    with open(output, "w") as f:
        for ide, ind in enumerate(pareto):
            genes = ''.join(str(i) for i in list(ind))   #
Encoded representation of the circuit
            gates, acc = ind.fitness.values  # Circuit
complexity and accuracy
            line = f'{ide},"{genes}",{gates},{acc}'
            f.write(line + '\n')
            print(line)
```

This function uses the `gsvm.gsvm` method to execute the
genetic algorithm, evolving circuits over multiple generations.
The results are saved to a file for further analysis.

You can run the genetic algorithm with:

```
# Starts the optimization process

evol()
```

The output includes the encoded representation of the circuits, their complexity (number of gates), and accuracy (or AUC, for which you need to change the computed metric in the functions defined in the repository).

Once the genetic algorithm finishes, results are sorted to identify the best-performing circuits. This involves reading the saved file and organizing the circuits based on accuracy and complexity.

```
# Read the genetic algorithm output

iot_result = pd.read_csv('sample_result.csv', header=None)

# Sort results by accuracy and circuit complexity

def ordenar_salidas_pareto(dataframe):
    dataframe.columns = ['ind', 'circ', 'gates', 'acc']  #
Name columns
    dataframe.sort_values(['acc', 'gates'], ascending=[False,
False], inplace=True)  # Sort by accuracy
    dataframe.reset_index(inplace=True)  # Reset index
    dataframe.pop('index')  # Remove old index
    return dataframe

# Process and display sorted results

iot_salidas = ordenar_salidas_pareto(iot_result)
print(iot_salidas)
```

The sorted dataframe prioritizes circuits with higher accuracy and lower complexity, simplifying the selection process for further evaluation.

The genetic algorithm outputs an encoded representation of circuits. These encodings are converted into executable quantum circuits using the CircuitConversor class.

```
from qiskit.circuit import QuantumCircuit, ParameterVector,
QuantumRegister
```

```
# Define a class to convert encoded circuits into Qiskit
quantum circuits

class CircuitConversor:
    def __init__(self, nqubits, nparameters):
        self.nqubits = nqubits
        self.x = ParameterVector('x', nparameters)  # Define
tunable parameters
        self.register = QuantumRegister(nqubits, 'q')  #
Quantum register
        self.gates = {  # Map encoded gates to quantum
operations
            '000': lambda qc, q: qc.h(q),  # Hadamard gate
            '001': lambda qc, q: qc.rx(self.x[0], q),  # RX
rotation
            '010': lambda qc, q: qc.ry(self.x[1], q),  # RY
rotation
            '011': lambda qc, q: qc.rz(self.x[2], q)  # RZ
rotation
        }

    # Generate the quantum circuit from encoded genes
    def __call__(self, coding):
        circuit = QuantumCircuit(self.register)  # Initialize
the circuit
        for i, gate_code in enumerate(coding):  # Apply gates
based on encoding
            qubit = i % self.nqubits
            self.gates[gate_code](circuit, qubit)
        return circuit
```

Then we create and visualize the circuit corresponding to the best-performing encoding:

```
# Instantiate the converter and generate the circuit

cc = CircuitConversor(nqubits=2, nparameters=3)
circuit = cc(iot_salidas['circ'][0])  # Convert the best
circuit
circuit.draw('mpl')  # Visualize the circuit
```

The optimized quantum circuit serves as the feature map for the QSVM. The circuit is integrated into a quantum kernel for classification.

```
from qiskit_machine_learning.kernels import QuantumKernel
from qiskit_machine_learning.algorithms import QSVC
from qiskit import Aer

# Set up the quantum kernel using the optimized circuit

backend = Aer.get_backend('qasm_simulator')  # Quantum
simulator
quantum_kernel = QuantumKernel(feature_map=circuit,
quantum_instance=backend)

# Train the QSVM on the optimized kernel

qsvc = QSVC(quantum_kernel=quantum_kernel, probability=True)
qsvc.fit(X_train, y_train)

# Evaluate the QSVM on test data

predictions = qsvc.predict(X_test)
```

This implementation demonstrates how genetic algorithms can optimize quantum feature maps for QSVMs, balancing accuracy and circuit complexity. By automating the design process, this approach reduces manual iteration steps and improves classification performance on nonlinear datasets.

On top of this approach, several others can be found that use the benefit of genetic algorithms to enhance the circuit definition. Usually improving performance, this shows how the quantum piece of your model architecture can be highly adaptable to the dataset being used.

Further Reading

Kernel methods in machine learning:
  https://arxiv.org/abs/math/0701907

Quantum-enhanced Versus Classical Support Vector
Machine: An Application to Stock Index Forecasting:
  https://papers.ssrn.com/sol3/papers.cfm?abstract_id=4630419

The complexity of quantum support vector machines:
  https://quantum-journal.org/papers/q-2024-01-11-1225/#

CVXPY library:
  https://www.cvxpy.org/

Kernel-based training of quantum models with scikit-learn:
  https://pennylane.ai/qml/demos/tutorial_kernel_based_training

Quantum Kernel Evaluation via Hong-Ou-Mandel
Interference:
  https://arxiv.org/abs/2212.12083

Experimental quantum-enhanced kernels on a photonic
processor:
  https://arxiv.org/abs/2407.20364

GA4QCO: Genetic Algorithm for Quantum Circuit
Optimization:
  https://arxiv.org/abs/2302.01303

Automatic design of quantum feature maps:
  https://arxiv.org/abs/2105.12626
  https://iopscience.iop.org/article/10.1088/2058-9565/ac1ab1
  https://github.com/sergio94al/Automatic_design_of_quantu
  m_feature_maps_Genetic_Auto-Generation

Chapter Figures

Figure 15: Kernel transformation of 2D data points into the 3D space
https://www.researchgate.net/publication/340610860_Multi-stage_Jamming_Attacks_Detection_using_Deep_Learning_Combined_with_Kernelized_Support_Vector_Machine_in_5G_Cloud_Radio_Access_Networks

Figure 16: Transformation of data from input space to classical and quantum feature spaces
https://www.researchgate.net/publication/373122191_Quantum-Enhanced_Support_Vector_Machine_for_Sentiment_Classification/figures?lo=1

Figure 17: Plotted heatmap illustrating the similarities between the dummies data points
GitHub repository, Chapter 7, *Multiple Kernel Alignement.ipynb* Jupyter notebook

Figure 18: Genetic algorithm technique workflow for optimizing the quantum feature map
https://iopscience.iop.org/article/10.1088/2058-9565/ac1ab1

CHAPTER 8

Variational Quantum Classifiers

Introduction

A Variational Quantum Classifier (VQC) is a QML model designed to classify data by leveraging parameterized quantum circuits. Unlike traditional quantum kernel methods, where the feature map is fixed, VQCs introduce trainable quantum circuits that can adapt to different datasets through optimization. This approach allows the classifier to adjust itself dynamically, improving its ability to separate classes in complex data patterns.

The key innovation of a VQC lies in its hybrid quantum-classical structure. The model consists of a quantum circuit that processes the data and a classical optimizer that fine-tunes the quantum parameters. The data is first mapped into a quantum state using an initial encoding, after which the quantum circuit transforms it using trainable gates. The outcome of the circuit is measured, producing a result that is fed into a classical machine learning framework. The classical component of the model then updates the quantum circuit's parameters to minimize classification error. This iterative loop goes on until the classifier achieves optimal performance.

VQCs are particularly appealing because they offer a degree of flexibility that static quantum feature maps do not. Instead of relying on predefined mappings that may or may not be suitable for a given dataset, a VQC actively learns the best way to separate different classes within the data. This ability to optimize quantum circuits makes VQCs a promising alternative to standard QSVMs, especially when working with high-dimensional or complex data structures where the optimal quantum representation is unknown and difficult to find.

One of the primary motivations for developing VQCs is their compatibility with NISQ devices. These quantum processors, while still limited in scale and coherence time, can support variational circuits due to their shallow depth and efficient use of qubits. By keeping quantum operations to their minimum and offloading computationally intensive tasks to classical optimization algorithms, VQCs provide a practical way to explore quantum-enhanced machine learning even before large-scale fault-tolerant quantum computers become available.

The effectiveness of a VQC depends on several factors, including the choice of the parameterized quantum circuit and the classical optimization strategy. Different circuit architectures introduce varying levels of entanglement and complexity, affecting the model's ability to distinguish data patterns. Additionally, training a VQC presents other challenges, such as vanishing gradients (barren plateaus) and noise-induced errors, which require careful selection of optimizers and training techniques.

In spite of these challenges, VQCs have shown potential in early experiments and theoretical studies. Researchers have applied them to problems spanning across image recognition, finance, and natural sciences, testing their ability to learn and generalize from data. While current implementations do not yet surpass classical machine learning models in performance, they provide valuable insights into how quantum circuits can be adapted for practical classification tasks. As quantum hardware improves and more efficient optimization methods are developed, VQCs may become a foundational tool in quantum machine learning, offering advantages over purely classical approaches in specific domains.

Classical and quantum working together

Training a VQC requires a careful interplay between quantum computations and classical optimization. The quantum part of the classifier is responsible for processing input data through a parameterized quantum circuit, where classical information is encoded into quantum states, transformed using quantum gates, and then measured to extract relevant features. However, the parameters of this quantum circuit are not static; they need to be optimized to improve classification accuracy, and this is where the classical part comes into place.

In a VQC, the optimization target is the best set of parameters for the quantum circuit, which minimizes a loss function, typically related to classification error. These parameters correspond to angles in quantum gates, which control how the qubits evolve and interact with each other. The optimization process consists of iteratively adjusting these angles to improve the classifier's ability to distinguish between different classes. However, unlike classical machine learning models where gradients can be computed directly, quantum circuits require additional steps. Quantum measurements introduce statistical fluctuations, meaning that the outputs are probabilistic rather than exact. Additionally, the nature of quantum mechanics prevents direct access to the internal states of qubits, making gradient computations less straightforward.

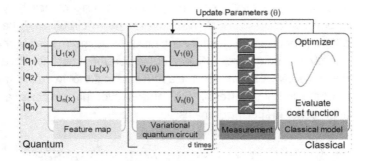

Figure 19: This diagram illustrates the hybrid quantum-classical workflow of a Variational Quantum Classifier (VQC). It shows the quantum feature mapping and variational circuit processing data, followed by classical optimization to update quantum circuit parameters iteratively. Source: https://medium.com/@typekrish/what-is-a-variational-quantum-classifier-888e40f83b24

To address these challenges, classical optimization methods are used to guide the learning process of the quantum classifier. These methods adjust the quantum circuit parameters based on the measured outputs, refining the circuit until it reaches an optimal configuration. Some of the most commonly used optimization techniques include gradient-based methods, which rely on estimating how small changes in quantum gate parameters affect the classification result, and gradient-free methods, which explore parameter space without requiring precise derivative calculations. For the classical optimizer, the quantum circuit is a black box, producing outputs that the optimizer uses to determine the next set of parameter updates.

Gradient-based methods attempt to leverage the structure of the quantum model by computing how the loss function changes with respect to each parameter in the circuit. Since direct differentiation is not possible in quantum systems, special techniques, such as the parameter shift rule, are employed to estimate gradients by evaluating the circuit at slightly different parameter values. These estimated gradients are then fed into classical optimizers like Adam or stochastic gradient descent, which update the parameters sequentially in the direction that reduces classification error. The advantage of this approach is that it allows for a more efficient search within the parameter space, enabling faster convergence. However, gradient-based optimization can struggle when quantum circuits become too deep, as the gradients tend to vanish, a problem known as barren plateaus, where updates become ineffective.

When working with real quantum hardware, noise and measurement uncertainty can make gradient calculations unreliable. This is where gradient-free methods become useful. These methods, such as COBYLA and evolutionary algorithms, do not require explicit gradients but instead adjust parameters based on trial evaluations of the circuit. They work by systematically exploring different parameter combinations, selecting those that improve performance, and iteratively refining the circuit. While these approaches are often more robust to quantum noise, they tend to require more evaluations to converge to a good solution, making them computationally expensive.

The interaction between the quantum and classical parts of a VQC is an iterative feedback loop. The quantum processor runs the circuit with a given set of parameters, producing measurement results. These results are passed to the classical optimizer, which analyzes them and determines how the quantum circuit should be adjusted. The updated parameters are then sent back to the quantum circuit for the next iteration, and the process repeats itself until the model stabilizes at an optimal configuration. This hybrid approach allows quantum models to leverage the strengths of both quantum computation—such as exploring high-dimensional feature spaces—and classical computation—such as efficiently optimizing complex functions.

Choosing the right optimization strategy is critical for VQCs to be effective in practice. If the quantum circuit is shallow, i.e., it has a small number of layers and parameters, gradient-based methods are usually preferred because they can converge quickly. However, as the number of parameters increases and noise becomes more pronounced, gradient-free methods may be more effective at navigating the optimization landscape. In many cases, hybrid strategies are used, where an initial phase of coarse searching is performed using a gradient-free approach, followed by fine-tuning with a gradient-based optimizer.

The overall success of a VQC depends not only on the power of the quantum circuit itself but also on how efficiently the classical optimizer can guide it toward a useful solution. As quantum hardware improves, new optimization techniques will likely emerge, which will be better suited for quantum learning tasks, making VQCs more practical for real-world applications. For now, the interaction between quantum circuits and classical optimizers remains a fascinating challenge, blending the strengths of both paradigms to push the boundaries of machine learning.

Autoencoders and their implications on VQC

The integration of autoencoders with VQCs is a remarkable step forward in the evolution of hybrid quantum-classical machine learning. This approach combines the strengths of classical neural networks, known for their ability to compress and distill data, with the unique power of quantum circuits to process data in high-dimensional feature spaces. By doing so, it not only addresses the limitations of current quantum hardware, but it also introduces new, more efficient ways of solving complex real-world problems.

At its core, an autoencoder is a type of neural network designed to encode input data into a smaller, more compact representation, referred to as the latent space, and then decode it back to reconstruct the original data. This compression is not arbitrary; the autoencoder learns how to preserve the most critical features of the data while discarding noise and redundant information. For instance, in the context of credit default prediction, an autoencoder can take a customer's financial history—a high-dimensional dataset with numerous features—and reduce it to a concise representation that captures the essential patterns needed to predict default risk. This latent space is smaller and more structured, making it an ideal input for a quantum circuit.

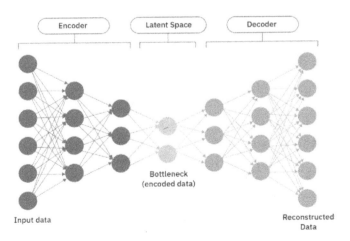

Figure 20: This image illustrates an autoencoder architecture, where the input data is compressed into a latent space (bottleneck) by the encoder and then reconstructed by the decoder. In the quantum context, the latent

space represents the essential features of the input data, which are then processed by a Variational Quantum Classifier (VQC) for classification tasks. Source: https://www.ibm.com/think/topics/variational-autoencoder

When these two technologies (autoencoders and VQCs) are combined, the result is a highly efficient and synergistic hybrid model. The autoencoder acts as a preprocessing step, preparing the data for quantum processing by reducing its dimensionality and filtering out irrelevant noise. By feeding only the most relevant features into the quantum circuit, the autoencoder ensures that the quantum resources are used optimally, focusing on extracting insights from the core patterns in the data.

The quantum circuit, in turn, takes these latent features and processes them within a quantum-enhanced feature space. By encoding the data into quantum states and applying parameterized transformations, the VQC amplifies the separability of classes within the dataset. For example, in a binary classification task such as predicting whether a customer will default or not, the quantum circuit transforms the latent features in a way that makes the two classes more distinguishable. This ability to explore complex, nonlinear relationships in the data gives the VQC a potential edge over classical classifiers, particularly for challenging datasets.

The training process for this hybrid model is where the true power of integration becomes evident. Both the autoencoder and the VQC are trained together in a unified framework, guided by a combined loss function that balances two objectives: minimizing reconstruction error and optimizing classification accuracy. The reconstruction error measures how well the autoencoder can rebuild the original data from its latent space, ensuring that the compressed representation retains all the essential information. Classification accuracy, on the other hand, evaluates how well the VQC distinguishes between different classes in the dataset. By optimizing these two objectives simultaneously, the model creates a latent space that is both compact and highly informative for the quantum classifier.

This iterative training process creates a feedback loop between the classical and quantum components. The autoencoder compresses the data, the VQC processes it and generates predictions, and the combined loss function evaluates the performance of the entire system. Based on this evaluation, the parameters of both the autoencoder and the quantum circuit are updated. This continuous interplay ensures that the latent space is not only efficient but also tailored to the strengths of the quantum classifier.

The integration of autoencoders and VQCs has several practical benefits. First, it significantly reduces the quantum hardware requirements by lowering the dimensionality of the input data. This makes them feasible to implement on today's NISQ devices, which are limited in both qubit count and coherence time. Second, it enhances the robustness of the quantum model by feeding it with cleaner and more structured data. The autoencoder's ability to filter out noise and highlight essential patterns ensures that the quantum circuit focuses on meaningful transformations, rather than being overwhelmed by irrelevant details.

In addition to addressing hardware limitations, this approach also unlocks new capabilities. The quantum circuit's ability to explore high-dimensional spaces complements the autoencoder's capacity for dimensionality reduction, creating a model that is both efficient and powerful. For example, in credit risk assessment, this hybrid model could identify subtle patterns in a customer's financial behavior that indicate an increased likelihood of default, even when those patterns are buried within a large and noisy dataset. By leveraging the unique strengths of quantum computation, the VQC provides insights that might be beyond the reach of purely classical methods.

Now let's dive deeper with a code example. First, we need to import the necessary libraries in Python.

```python
import pandas as pd
import numpy as np
from sklearn.model_selection import train_test_split
from sklearn.preprocessing import MinMaxScaler
from sklearn.metrics import roc_auc_score
from sklearn.decomposition import PCA
import matplotlib.pyplot as plt
import torch
import torch.nn as nn
import pennylane as qml
```

The preprocessing steps prepare the data for machine learning models.

```python
# Import your dataset

df = pd.read_csv('yourdataset.csv')



# Split into features (X) and labels (y)

X = df.drop(['target'], axis="columns")
y = df['target']



# Create training and testing splits

X_train, X_test, y_train, y_test = train_test_split(X, y,
test_size=0.20, random_state=42)
```

```
# Normalize feature values to range [0, 1]

scaler = MinMaxScaler()
X_train = scaler.fit_transform(X_train)
X_test = scaler.transform(X_test)
```

The X variables (features) are separated from the y variable (labels), and then splitted into train and test sets. The normalization step, using `MinMaxScaler`, ensures that all features are scaled to the same range, preventing features with larger numeric ranges from dominating others. This step is particularly important for neural networks and quantum circuits, as they perform better with normalized inputs. Remember to fit only on the train set, and transform the test set with this previously-computed fit.

As mentioned before, the autoencoder is a neural network designed to compress high-dimensional input data into a lower-dimensional representation, latent space, and reconstruct the original input from this compressed form. This step helps reduce the complexity of the input before it's fed into the quantum circuit.

```
class Autoencoder(nn.Module):
        def __init__(self, input_dim, latent_dim):
                super(Autoencoder, self).__init__()
                self.encoder = nn.Sequential(
                        nn.Linear(input_dim, 128),    # First
layer reduces dimensionality

                        nn.ReLU(),    # Activation adds non-
linearity
                        nn.Linear(128, 64),    # Second layer
further compresses
                        nn.ReLU(),
                        nn.Linear(64, latent_dim)    # Latent
space representation
                )
                self.decoder = nn.Sequential(
```

```
                        nn.Linear(latent_dim, 64),  # Reverse
compression in decoder
                        nn.ReLU(),
                        nn.Linear(64, 128),
                        nn.ReLU(),
                        nn.Linear(128,     input_dim)        #
Reconstruct original input
                )

        def forward(self, x):
                z = self.encoder(x)  # Encoded representation
                x_reconstructed  =  self.decoder(z)        #
Reconstructed input
                return z, x_reconstructed
```

The encoder compresses the input features into a compact latent representation with 4 dimensions. This latent space captures the most important patterns in the data. The decoder then reconstructs the original features from this compressed representation, ensuring that it retains meaningful information. This step reduces the input complexity for the quantum circuit and helps highlight the most relevant features.

The quantum circuit processes the latent features produced by the autoencoder.

```
#Quantum circuit definition

#Number of qubits to process the latent space

n_qubits = 2

#Latent space matches the number of qubits

latent_dim = 2

#Number of layers in the circuit
```

```
n_layers = 3

def quantum_circuit(params, features):
        qml.AngleEmbedding(features, wires=range(n_qubits),
rotation='Y')  # Encode features into qubit states
        for layer in range(n_layers):
                for i in range(n_qubits):  # Apply RY
rotation gates
                        qml.RY(params[layer, i], wires=i)
                for i in range(n_qubits - 1):  # Add
entanglement between adjacent qubits
                        qml.CNOT(wires=[i, i + 1])
                qml.CNOT(wires=[n_qubits - 1, 0])  # Add
entanglement between the last and first qubits
        return qml.expval(qml.PauliZ(0))  # Measure the
expectation value of the first qubit
```

The circuit first maps the latent features into quantum states using AngleEmbedding, where each feature rotates a qubit around the Y-axis. The circuit then applies three layers of transformations, each consisting of parameterized rotation gates (RY) and entangling CNOT gates. These transformations create a complex quantum state that amplifies separability in the data.

To integrate the quantum circuit with PyTorch, we define a quantum node and build the VQC model.

```
# Define a quantum simulator device


dev = qml.device("default.qubit", wires=n_qubits)

# Define the quantum node for PyTorch
@qml.qnode(dev, interface='torch')
def quantum_node(features, params):
        return quantum_circuit(params, features)

class VQC(nn.Module):
        def __init__(self, latent_dim, n_qubits, n_layers):
                super(VQC, self).__init__()
```

```
                    self.latent_dim = latent_dim
                    self.n_qubits = n_qubits
                    self.params =
nn.Parameter(torch.randn(n_layers, n_qubits,
dtype=torch.float64))  # Trainable circuit parameters
                    self.sigmoid = nn.Sigmoid()  # Ensure output
is between 0 and 1

        def forward(self, x):
                    x_split = torch.chunk(x,
chunks=self.latent_dim // self.n_qubits, dim=1)  # Split
features for qubits
                    outputs = [quantum_node(x_sub, self.params)
for x_sub in x_split]  # Process each chunk
                    raw_output = torch.stack(outputs,
dim=1).mean(dim=1, keepdim=True)  # Aggregate outputs
                    return self.sigmoid(raw_output)
```

The quantum node runs the quantum circuit with latent features as input and outputs a probability. The VQC splits the latent features into chunks that can fit within the available qubits and processes each chunk independently.

Now, we integrate the autoencoder and VQC into a unified hybrid model.

```
#Combined loss function

class GuidedQuantumCompression(nn.Module):
        def __init__(self, autoencoder, vqc, lambda_param):
                super(GuidedQuantumCompression,
self).__init__()
                    self.autoencoder = autoencoder
                    self.vqc = vqc
                    self.lambda_param = lambda_param
                    self.mse_loss = nn.MSELoss()  # Loss for
autoencoder reconstruction
                    self.bce_loss = nn.BCELoss()  # Loss for VQC
classification

        def forward(self, x, y):
                    z, x_reconstructed = self.autoencoder(x)  #
```

```
Compress input                        y_pred = self.vqc(z)   #
Classify latent representation
                reconstruction_loss =
self.mse_loss(x_reconstructed, x)   # Measure reconstruction
quality
                classification_loss = self.bce_loss(y_pred,
y)   # Measure classification performance
                return (1 - self.lambda_param) *
reconstruction_loss + self.lambda_param * classification_loss
```

This combined model trains both components simultaneously. The `lambda_param` determines the balance between reconstructing the input and correctly classifying the output.

The training loop optimizes the autoencoder and VQC parameters.

```
#Model initialization

input_dim = X_train.shape[1] # Number of features in input
data
lambda_param = 0.5 # Balances reconstruction loss and
classification loss

# Initialize the Autoencoder and Variational Quantum
Classifier (VQC)
autoencoder = Autoencoder(input_dim, latent_dim).double()
vqc = VQC(latent_dim, n_qubits, n_layers).double()
model = GuidedQuantumCompression(autoencoder, vqc,
lambda_param).double()

#Optimizer
optimizer = torch.optim.Adam(model.parameters(), lr=0.001)

batch_size = 32
X_train_tensor = torch.tensor(X_train, dtype=torch.float64)
y_train_tensor = torch.tensor(y_train.values,
dtype=torch.float64).view(-1, 1)

data_loader = torch.utils.data.DataLoader(
```

```
        dataset=torch.utils.data.TensorDataset(X_train_tensor
, y_train_tensor),
        batch_size=batch_size,
        shuffle=True
)

#Training loop with 100 epochs
loss_history = []
n_epochs = 100
for epoch in range(n_epochs):
        total_loss = 0
        reconstruction_loss = 0
        classification_loss = 0
        for batch_x, batch_y in data_loader:
                optimizer.zero_grad()
                # Forward pass: Encode input data into latent
        space and reconstruct it
                z, x_reconstructed = autoencoder(batch_x)
                # Classify the latent representation using the
        quantum classifier
                y_pred = vqc(z)

                recon_loss  =  nn.MSELoss()(x_reconstructed,
batch_x)  #  Reconstruction  loss  (MSE  between  input  and
reconstructed data)
                class_loss = model.bce_loss(y_pred, batch_y)
# Classification loss (Binary Cross-Entropy)
                # Weighted sum of losses based on lambda_param
                loss = (1 - lambda_param) * recon_loss +
lambda_param * class_loss

                loss.backward()
                optimizer.step()

                total_loss += loss.item()
                reconstruction_loss += recon_loss.item()
                classification_loss += class_loss.item()
                loss_history.append(total_loss)
                print(f"Epoch {epoch + 1}/{n_epochs}, Total
Loss: {total_loss:.4f}, "
                f"Reconstruction                    Loss:
{reconstruction_loss:.4f},        Classification        Loss:
{classification_loss:.4f}")
```

During each epoch, the model processes small batches of data, calculates the loss function, and updates its parameters. This iterative process ensures the autoencoder and VQC improve over time.

Finally, the model is evaluated on the test set.

```
# Compress test data


X_test_tensor = torch.tensor(X_test, dtype=torch.float64)

y_test_tensor = torch.tensor(y_test.values,
dtype=torch.float64).view(-1, 1)
z_test, _ = autoencoder(torch.tensor(X_test,
dtype=torch.float64))

# Classify compressed test data

preds = vqc(z_test)  # Classify compressed test data

# Evaluate using AUC

auc_score = roc_auc_score(y_test, preds.detach().numpy())
```

The test data is compressed into the latent space and classified using the VQC. The AUC score measures how well the model distinguishes between defaulting and non-defaulting customers.

Further Reading

Variational Quantum Algorithms:
   https://arxiv.org/abs/2012.09265

Variational quantum algorithms: fundamental concepts, applications and challenges:
   https://link.springer.com/article/10.1007/s11128-024-04438-2

Variational classifier:
https://pennylane.ai/qml/demos/tutorial_variational_classifier

Image Classification with Rotation-Invariant Variational Quantum Circuits:
https://arxiv.org/html/2403.15031v1

(DEMO) QViSTA: A Novel Quantum Vision Transformer for Early Multi-Stage Alzheimer's Diagnosis Using Optimized Variational Quantum Circuits:
https://openreview.net/forum?id=D9wNOMsMN6

Vanishing Gradient Mitigation with Deep Learning Neural Network Optimization:
https://ieeexplore.ieee.org/document/8843652

Parameter-shift Rule:
https://pennylane.ai/qml/glossary/parameter_shift

General parameter-shift rules for quantum gradients:
https://quantum-journal.org/papers/q-2022-03-30-677/

Barren plateaus in quantum neural networks:
https://pennylane.ai/qml/demos/tutorial_barren_plateaus

Diagnosing Barren Plateaus with Tools from Quantum Optimal Control:
https://quantum-journal.org/papers/q-2022-09-29-824/

Escaping from the Barren Plateau via Gaussian Initializations in Deep Variational Quantum Circuits:
https://arxiv.org/abs/2203.09376

Gradient-free optimizers – COBYLA:
https://openqaoa.entropicalabs.com/optimizers/gradient-free-optimizers/#cobyla

---

Enhancing the performance of Variational Quantum Classifiers with hybrid autoencoders:
   https://arxiv.org/html/2409.03350v1

Neural Discrete Representation Learning:
   https://arxiv.org/abs/1711.00937

Chapter Figures

Figure 19: Diagram of the hybrid quantum-classical workflow of a VQC
   https://medium.com/@typekrish/what-is-a-variational-quantum-classifier-888e40f83b24

Figure 20: Autoencoder architecture
   https://www.ibm.com/think/topics/variational-autoencoder

CHAPTER 9

Promising Approaches

Introduction

As QML continues to evolve, the need for more scalable, efficient, and robust techniques becomes increasingly evident. While foundational methods such as QSVM and VQC have demonstrated the potential of quantum-enhanced learning, they also highlight several key challenges—data encoding bottlenecks, optimization difficulties, and model scalability. In this chapter, we explore approaches that push beyond these limitations, presenting techniques that enhance the practicality and efficiency of QML models.

One of the central themes we'll explore is optimization, a crucial aspect of training quantum models. We'll revisit metaheuristic optimization schemes, which leverage evolutionary strategies and search algorithms to improve quantum model performance. These approaches provide alternative ways to navigate complex loss landscapes, offering solutions where traditional optimizers struggle. Alongside this, we examine QUBO-based SVM, a reformulation of classical support vector machines into quantum-friendly quadratic unconstrained binary optimization (QUBO) problems, which allow quantum processors to efficiently handle classification tasks.

Beyond optimization, we delve into novel computational architectures such as quantum reservoir computing, which harnesses the dynamic behavior of quantum systems to process and transform data without requiring extensive training. This approach is particularly valuable for tasks involving temporal sequences and complex dependencies. Additionally, we explore Quantum Neural Networks (QNNs), which integrate quantum circuits into deep learning paradigms.

Data representation and encoding are also central to scalable QML, and we examine innovative techniques such as bit-bit encoding and sub-net initialization. These strategies address challenges in quantum data loading and parameter initialization, ensuring that models are not hindered by barren plateaus or inefficient feature embeddings. We further analyze optimizer-free training techniques that allow quantum models to converge without the reliance on traditional classical optimizers.

Throughout this chapter, we aim to provide a comprehensive exploration of these QML techniques, discussing their theoretical underpinnings, practical implications, and potential applications.

Reservoir computing

As we previously explored in Chapter 3, Quantum Reservoir Computing (QRC) is a promising framework for processing information using the inherent complexity of quantum systems. It's inspired by classical reservoir computing, a paradigm used in recurrent neural networks (RNNs) where a static, randomly initialized system (the reservoir) transforms input data into a higher-dimensional feature space. This transformation enables simpler, often linear models to extract meaningful patterns from complex datasets. In the quantum domain, QRC utilizes a quantum system as a reservoir, leveraging quantum properties to enhance the expressivity of the feature space. This approach is particularly useful for QML, as it allows classical data to be embedded into a quantum system, processed through a quantum reservoir, and then interpreted by a classical model.

The quantum reservoir itself is constructed using a quantum circuit that consists of randomly applied rotation gates and controlled operations that create entanglement between qubits. This randomness is intentional; it acts as a non-trainable feature extractor, allowing the quantum system to naturally evolve into a rich state that encodes the input data in a high-dimensional quantum space. The circuit depth, which controls the number of transformations applied to the quantum system, determines the complexity of this encoding process. By introducing multiple layers of random quantum operations, the reservoir captures intricate relationships within the input data, making it easier for a classical model to extract meaningful insights.

Once the input data has been mapped into the quantum reservoir, measurements are performed on the quantum circuit to extract feature representations. Each qubit's measurement provides a probability distribution over its possible states, which serves as the transformed feature set for downstream processing. Because quantum measurement collapses the wavefunction into classical outcomes, multiple runs (shots) are required to estimate these probabilities accurately. This process effectively maps classical input data into a nonlinear quantum feature space, where patterns that might be difficult to discern in the original representation become more apparent.

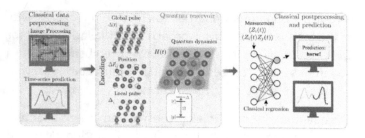

Figure 21: Quantum Reservoir Computing (QRC) maps classical data into a quantum system, evolving it through quantum dynamics to generate high-dimensional embeddings. These quantum-transformed features are then processed by classical machine learning models for efficient pattern recognition and inference. Source: https://arxiv.org/abs/2407.02553

After extracting quantum reservoir features, a classical linear regression model is trained to interpret these transformed features and make predictions. This hybrid approach—where quantum circuits are used for feature extraction while a classical model is used for decision-making—highlights one of the key advantages of quantum machine learning in the near term. Instead of requiring an end-to-end quantum model, QRC allows existing classical models to benefit from the enhanced representational power of quantum systems without the need for extensive quantum hardware like when we are using quantum kernels.

QRC is particularly useful in scenarios where conventional methods struggle with feature extraction due to high-dimensional or highly nonlinear relationships in the data. Unlike traditional quantum algorithms that require extensive optimization and parameter tuning, QRC leverages the natural evolution of quantum states, making it a robust and efficient tool for qQML. It offers a scalable way to integrate quantum systems with classical machine learning models, providing a glimpse into how quantum-enhanced feature processing can become a valuable asset for real-world applications.

Before we dive into executing the quantum reservoir, we need to define the structure of the quantum system that will act as our reservoir. Random rotations and entanglements will be used to set up the reservoir so that the input data can go through a rich quantum transformation.

The idea behind this step is similar to a classical reservoir computing model, where a randomly initialized recurrent neural network (RNN) transforms input data into a higher-dimensional feature space.

Let's initialize the quantum reservoir by creating a quantum circuit with a fixed depth of transformations.

```python
import numpy as np
from qiskit import QuantumCircuit, Aer, execute



def create_quantum_reservoir(num_qubits, depth):
        """
        A quantum reservoir with random rotations and
entanglement.
        :param num_qubits: Number of qubits in the reservoir.
        :param depth: Number of layers in the reservoir
circuit.
        :return: QuantumCircuit object.
        """

        qc = QuantumCircuit(num_qubits)
        np.random.seed(42)  # Ensure reproducibility

        for _ in range(depth):
                for qubit in range(num_qubits):
                        qc.rx(np.random.uniform(0, 2 *
np.pi), qubit)  # Random X-rotation
                for qubit in range(num_qubits - 1):
                        qc.cx(qubit, qubit + 1)  # Introduce
entanglement
        return qc
```

Here, we are doing two key things:

- Applying random rotations to each qubit using `qc.rx()`. This simulates how classical neural networks introduce non-linearity using activation functions.
- Creating entanglements using `qc.cx()`, which helps spread information across the quantum system, ensuring that data is not only transformed independently per qubit but also in combination.

Now that we have the quantum reservoir, we need to inject classical data into the system so that it can undergo transformation. To do this, we encode data using Y-rotations.

```
def encode_input(qc, data, num_qubits):
    """
    Encode classical data into the quantum circuit.
    :param qc: QuantumCircuit object.
    :param data: List of input values.
    :param num_qubits: Number of qubits in the reservoir.
    """

    for i, value in enumerate(data):
        qc.ry(value, i % num_qubits)  # Encode data
using Y-rotation
```

This function modifies the state of the qubits based on the classical input data. The value of each feature determines how much the qubit rotates along the Y-axis.

After encoding data into the quantum reservoir, we need to execute the quantum circuit and extract meaningful features. In quantum computing, measurements collapse quantum states into classical values, which means we need multiple runs (shots) to estimate meaningful distributions.

```
def run_reservoir(qc, num_qubits):
        """
        Simulate the quantum reservoir and extract features
from measurements.
        :param qc: QuantumCircuit object.
        :param num_qubits: Number of qubits.
        :return: Feature vector (measurement probabilities).
        """

        backend = Aer.get_backend('qasm_simulator')
        qc.measure_all()  # Add measurement gates
        result = execute(qc, backend, shots=200).result()  #
Simulate with 200 shots
        counts = result.get_counts()

        # Normalize counts to get probabilities

        probabilities = []
        for i in range(2 ** num_qubits):
                state = bin(i)[2:].zfill(num_qubits)  #
Convert index to binary string
                probabilities.append(counts.get(state, 0) /
200)
        return probabilities
```

This function executes the Qiskit Aer simulator, performs measurements on all qubits, and collects the probability distribution of quantum states. The result is a set of extracted quantum features that represent the transformed input data.

Now that we have all the necessary components, we can apply the quantum reservoir to transform our classical dataset into quantum-enhanced features.

```
# Parameters for Quantum Reservoir

num_qubits = 4   # We use 4 qubits for encoding
depth = 8        # Depth of quantum reservoir circuit
```

```
# Extract features from the quantum reservoir

def extract_quantum_features(data, num_qubits, depth):
        features = []
        for sample in data:
                qc = create_quantum_reservoir(num_qubits,
depth)
                encode_input(qc, sample, num_qubits)
        features.append(run_reservoir(qc, num_qubits))
        return np.array(features)

# Using LDA-transformed features for quantum reservoir

X_train_quantum = extract_quantum_features(X_train,
num_qubits, depth)X_test_quantum =
extract_quantum_features(X_test, num_qubits, depth)
```

Each sample in the dataset is passed through the quantum
reservoir, which transforms it into a quantum feature space.
This mapping allows quantum operations to enhance the
expressivity of the feature set.

At this point, we have successfully extracted quantum
features from our dataset. Now, we use a classical model
(Linear Regression) to classify the transformed data.

```
from sklearn.linear_model import LinearRegression
from sklearn.metrics import accuracy_score, roc_auc_score,
roc_curve



# Train a Linear Regression model

model = LinearRegression()
model.fit(X_train_quantum, y_train)

# Predict and evaluate

y_pred = model.predict(X_test_quantum)
y_pred_binary = (y_pred > 0.5).astype(int)  # Convert to binary
```

```
predictions
accuracy = accuracy_score(y_test, y_pred_binary)
print(f"Test Accuracy: {accuracy * 100:.2f}%")

# Calculate AUC

auc = roc_auc_score(y_test, y_pred)
print(f"Test AUC: {auc}")

# Calculate KS Statistic

fpr, tpr, _ = roc_curve(y_test, y_pred)
ks_stat = max(tpr - fpr)
print(f"Test KS Statistic: {ks_stat}")
```

This hybrid approach—where quantum-enhanced features are used by a classical learning algorithm—is a practical way of leveraging quantum computation in machine learning without requiring a full quantum model.

This implementation showcases a hybrid quantum-classical approach, where a quantum reservoir is used to extract complex feature representations, and a classical model is used for classification. The advantage of this approach is that we can leverage quantum computing's expressivity without requiring a fully quantum model. By incorporating quantum reservoirs, we explore how quantum-enhanced features can potentially outperform traditional classical feature extraction techniques, making this an exciting direction for future applications of QML.

Other techniques

Every week, new approaches emerge in preprints and academic journals, offering fresh perspectives on improving kernel methods, variational circuits, and hybrid quantum-classical architectures. The central challenge—what many consider the "elephant in the room" of QML—is finding strategies that make quantum models not only theoretically compelling but also practically advantageous over their classical counterparts.

In this section, we won't attempt to cover every single development—keeping up with that would require a book that never ends. Instead, we'll explore a few carefully chosen techniques that highlight key trends in the field. These methods are not necessarily "final solutions" but rather stepping stones that push QML forward, providing glimpses of where the field might be heading. Some focus on overcoming well-known obstacles like barren plateaus and trainability issues, while others rethink how quantum circuits encode data or optimize model parameters.

QUBO-based SVM

QUBO-based SVMs integrate quantum optimization techniques to enhance classification by reformulating the problem into a QUBO model. In this case, traditional SVMs rely on solving a constrained quadratic optimization problem to determine support vectors, which define the optimal decision boundary for classification. However, this classical approach can become computationally expensive, especially when handling large datasets or high-dimensional feature spaces. By leveraging quantum computing, the optimization problem is translated into a QUBO formulation, where finding the optimal support vectors is equivalent to minimizing a cost function encoded in a quantum system. This method capitalizes on quantum parallelism, allowing quantum processors to explore multiple configurations simultaneously, potentially leading to faster convergence and better solutions for complex data structures.

The QUBO matrix is built by encoding pairwise interactions between training samples, considering their labels and feature similarities. A regularization parameter is introduced to balance the trade-off between margin maximization and misclassification tolerance. The resulting QUBO formulation is then mapped onto a quantum hardware or simulator (usually depending on how many samples are being used for training purposes). The quantum reservoir undergoes an adiabatic evolution, where an initial quantum state is gradually transformed to encode the optimal solution. Measurements from this quantum process yield a binary solution that identifies which training samples should be considered as support vectors.

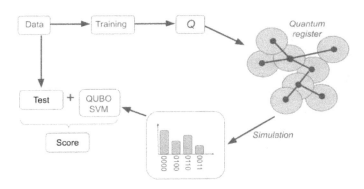

Figure 22: The diagram represents the process of training a Support Vector Machine (SVM) using a Quadratic Unconstrained Binary Optimization (QUBO) formulation, where the optimization problem is mapped to a quantum register for processing. After quantum simulation, the measured results are used to construct an SVM decision boundary, which is then tested on new data to evaluate the model's performance. Source: https://arxiv.org/abs/2409.11876

Once the quantum solver selects the support vectors, the next step is to compute the weight vector and bias term for the decision boundary. The weights are determined by summing the contributions of selected support vectors, weighted by their respective labels and optimization parameters. The bias is stabilized by taking the median of differences between the predicted and actual labels. To ensure robustness, parallelized classical post-processing is applied to evaluate the model's performance on the test dataset.

In the context of an SVM, weight and bias play a crucial role in defining how the model makes decisions. Think of weight as the importance assigned to each feature in the dataset. When a machine learning model processes data, it needs to understand which features are more relevant for distinguishing between different categories. The weight represents this influence—higher weights mean that a particular feature has a stronger impact on the final classification, while lower weights indicate less significance.

In other words, the weight determines how a hyperplane is positioned and tilted based on the data points. However, weight alone is not enough to fully describe the separation. This is where bias comes in. Bias is like an adjustable setting that shifts the entire decision boundary up or down, ensuring that the hyperplane is optimally placed to separate the two groups.

In the case of a QUBO-based SVM, the quantum optimizer selects certain data points—called support vectors—that are crucial in defining the classification boundary. The weight is calculated based on these support vectors, and the bias is then adjusted to make sure the decision boundary is as accurate as possible. In simple terms, weight tells us which features matter most, and bias fine-tunes the model's decision-making process to ensure the best possible classification of new data points.

This QUBO-based approach to SVM classification demonstrates the synergy between quantum and classical computation again. While the feature engineering and final classification steps remain classical, the computationally demanding optimization task is delegated to a quantum solver, offering potential advantages in scalability and efficiency. The method is particularly well-suited for datasets with small and complex structures where classical solvers may struggle due to local minima or high computational cost. By utilizing a quantum-enabled optimization framework, this hybrid approach provides a promising alternative to conventional SVMs, highlighting the potential of quantum machine learning for real-world classification problems.

Metaheuristic optimization scheme

Metaheuristic optimization schemes are a class of powerful search algorithms designed to solve complex optimization problems where traditional gradient-based methods struggle. These approaches do not require explicit derivatives, making them well-suited for problems with highly nonlinear, non-convex, or discrete solution spaces. In quantum machine learning, metaheuristic optimization is particularly relevant due to the nature of quantum circuits, where the placement of gates, their types, and the connections between qubits determine the effectiveness of quantum feature maps. Finding the optimal configuration for such circuits is challenging, as there is an enormous search space of possible structures and parameter settings. This is where metaheuristic techniques, such as genetic algorithms (GAs), become invaluable.

In the case presented here a GA is employed to optimize a quantum feature map used within a QSVC. The primary goal is to identify the most effective quantum circuit architecture for encoding classical data into quantum states in a way that maximizes classification performance. The GA mimics the process of natural selection by iteratively improving a population of candidate solutions. Each candidate, or individual, represents a possible quantum circuit configuration, including its rotation gates, entanglement operations, and parameterized quantum transformations. Over multiple generations, the GA evolves these circuits by selecting the best-performing ones, recombining their characteristics, and introducing mutations to explore new variations.

Each individual is encoded as a binary string that determines which quantum gates will be applied and how qubits will be connected. This encoding scheme defines the rotation gates (such as RX, RY, and RZ) and entanglement gates (such as CNOT, CZ, or SWAP) that will be used to construct the quantum feature map. The GA evaluates each circuit by constructing the corresponding quantum kernel function, which measures the similarity between quantum states. This kernel is then used to train an SVM, a classical machine learning model that finds an optimal decision boundary between different classes.

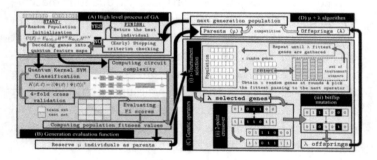

Figure 23: The image depicts a genetic algorithm (GA) optimizing quantum kernel SVM classification, evolving quantum feature maps through selection, crossover, and mutation. It integrates quantum circuit complexity assessment and fitness evaluation to refine the best-performing model. Source: https://onlinelibrary.wiley.com/doi/full/10.4218/etrij.2024-0144

The fitness function in the GA is designed to assess both the classification accuracy of the quantum-enhanced SVM and the complexity of the quantum circuit. At the same time, circuit complexity is factored into the fitness score to ensure that the resulting quantum feature map is not only effective but also efficient, reducing unnecessary quantum operations that might introduce noise or increase execution time.

After evaluating the initial population, the GA performs selection, crossover, and mutation to create the next generation of quantum circuits. The selection process chooses the best-performing circuits, favoring those with higher classification accuracy and lower complexity. The crossover operation then combines elements of two parent circuits, generating new offspring circuits that inherit characteristics from both. Finally, the mutation step introduces small random modifications, ensuring diversity in the population and preventing the algorithm from getting stuck in local optima.

This evolutionary process continues for multiple generations, refining the quantum feature maps over time. Once the GA converges to an optimal circuit, the best solution is extracted and used to compute the full kernel matrix for the dataset. The final SVM model is then trained using this optimized quantum kernel, and predictions can be made on test data.

One of the key advantages of using a metaheuristic approach like GA is its ability to automate the design of quantum feature maps. Traditional QML models often require manual tuning of circuit structures and parameters, which can be impractical given the vast number of possible configurations. By leveraging an evolutionary approach, this method systematically discovers better quantum circuit architectures, reducing human effort while improving classification performance. A similar approach was mentioned in Chapter 7 where GA was included in the context of measuring the accuracy and complexity of the feature map.

Overall, these metaheuristic optimization schemes provide an efficient and scalable way to tailor quantum circuits to specific datasets, ensuring that the quantum component contributes meaningfully to machine learning tasks. As quantum hardware continues to improve, these optimization techniques will play a crucial role in making quantum machine learning models more practical and competitive against classical alternatives.

A lot more techniques

The previous approaches highlighted in this chapter are selected due to promising tests realized by myself, but several other techniques are being explored in recent years to deal with one of the most pressing concerns in QML, which is the scalability problem. This arises due to data encoding bottlenecks, inefficient optimization strategies, and barren plateaus—regions of the optimization landscape where gradients vanish, making learning infeasible. To tackle these challenges, alternatives like bit-bit encoding have been proposed as an alternative to traditional quantum feature maps. Instead of representing input features as continuous values embedded into quantum states, bit-bit encoding directly encodes both input and output as binary strings. This method not only reduces the complexity of quantum data loading but also allows for unrestricted model expressivity while relying on classical preprocessing techniques to compress high-dimensional datasets into the most predictive degrees of freedom. By leveraging bit-bit encoding, QML models can become more practical for large-scale applications without requiring excessive quantum resources.

Another innovative approach is optimizer-free training, which redefines how quantum models are trained. In classical deep learning, gradient-based optimizers, such as Adam or stochastic gradient descent, are essential for minimizing loss functions. However, in quantum models, these optimizers often struggle due to noise, parameter dependency, and non-convex landscapes. Optimizer-free training circumvents this issue by updating only one parameter at a time in a deterministic way, ensuring convergence to a local minimum. Unlike classical training methods that require gradient descent with backpropagation, this quantum alternative provides a stable and structured approach to learning that is inherently resilient to barren plateaus. This method represents a fundamental shift in how quantum models can be trained, offering a clear advantage over classical approaches in certain scenarios.

Closely related to this is the sub-net initialization technique, which provides a practical way to overcome barren plateaus. In traditional QML, initializing a model with randomly assigned parameters often leads to poor performance, as gradients quickly vanish during training. Sub-net initialization addresses this by starting with a smaller, more compact quantum model trained on reduced data, and then using its optimized parameters to initialize a larger model with more qubits. This hierarchical approach ensures that as models scale, they inherit well-trained parameters from their smaller counterparts, significantly improving trainability. This method is particularly useful in hybrid quantum-classical machine learning workflows, where small quantum models can be efficiently trained and gradually expanded.

Another critical factor influencing the performance of quantum models is data-induced randomness. The way data is embedded into quantum states plays a crucial role in determining how well a model can distinguish between different classes. Poorly chosen embeddings can introduce excessive randomness, limiting a model's ability to learn meaningful patterns. To address this, researchers have introduced a metric called class margin, which quantifies the relationship between data-induced randomness and classification accuracy. By measuring the class margin, it's possible to evaluate whether a given data embedding strategy is likely to succeed before running extensive experiments. This approach provides a systematic way to select the best quantum data encoding methods, ensuring that models are trained on representations that maximize class separation and minimize unnecessary randomness.

Also, we cannot leave behind the QNNs. Hybrid QNN models offer a solution by offloading certain computations to classical processors while reserving quantum computation for operations that benefit most from quantum speedup, such as matrix multiplications, nonlinear transformations, and feature extraction. Classical systems handle tasks like data preprocessing and parameter updates, while quantum circuits execute the core learning process.

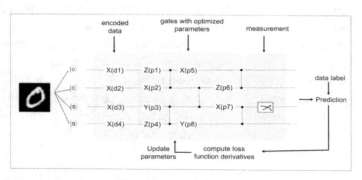

Figure 24: A Quantum Neural Network (QNN) architecture illustrating the process of data encoding, the application of parameterized quantum gates, and measurement operations for image classification, with parameters being adjusted through loss function optimization. Source: https://arxiv.org/abs/2501.09528

The design and training of QNNs introduce unique challenges not present in classical deep learning. Unlike conventional networks, where gradient-based optimization methods like backpropagation are well-established, quantum models require parameterized quantum circuits (PQCs) that evolve under quantum gates. These circuits introduce trainable parameters, which must be optimized to minimize loss functions. However, QNNs face the issue of barren plateaus, making optimization difficult. To address this, researchers have explored strategies like variational quantum algorithms (VQAs) and equivariant quantum networks, which tailor circuit architectures to the symmetries in the data, improving training stability and efficiency. Additionally, emerging theories suggest that overparameterization in QNNs—adding more quantum parameters than strictly necessary—can paradoxically improve learning capacity while preventing overfitting, a departure from classical machine learning principles.

Taken together, these approaches form a growing ecosystem of quantum machine learning techniques that aim to overcome the current limitations of quantum hardware and algorithms. By addressing fundamental challenges such as data encoding, optimization stability, barren plateaus, scalability, and randomness in classification, these methods pave the way for more scalable and practical quantum learning systems.

Further Reading

Quantum Machine Learning: An Applied Approach:
https://www.springerprofessional.de/en/quantum-machine-learning-an-applied-approach/19403222

Quantum Reservoir Computing:
https://www.quera.com/glossary/quantum-reservoir-computing

Quantum Reservoir Computing Tutorials by QuEra:
https://github.com/QuEraComputing/QRC-tutorials

Support vector machine based on the quadratic unconstrained binary optimization model:
https://iopscience.iop.org/article/10.1088/1742-6596/2858/1/012002

Metaheuristic optimization scheme for quantum kernel classifiers using entanglement-directed graphs:
https://onlinelibrary.wiley.com/doi/full/10.4218/etrij.2024-0144

Bit-bit encoding, optimizer-free training and sub-net initialization: techniques for scalable quantum machine learning:
https://arxiv.org/abs/2501.02148

Scalable quantum neural networks by few quantum resources:
https://arxiv.org/abs/2307.01017

Improved Financial Forecasting via Quantum Machine Learning:
https://arxiv.org/html/2306.12965v2

Chapter Figures

Figure 21: Example workflow of Quantum Reservoir
Computing (QRC)
   https://arxiv.org/abs/2407.02553

Figure 22: Training an SVM using Quadratic Unconstrained
Binary Optimization (QUBO) formulation
   https://arxiv.org/abs/2409.11876

Figure 23: Workflow of a Genetic Algorithm (GA) optimizing
a quantum kernel SVM classification
   https://onlinelibrary.wiley.com/doi/full/10.4218/etrij.2024-
   0144

Figure 24: A quantum neural network architecture
   https://arxiv.org/abs/2501.09528

CHAPTER 10

A Journey to Implement Yourself

Introduction

We explored a variety of quantum machine learning techniques throughout this book, examining their applications, challenges, and advantages when used alongside classical methods. Now, it's time to put everything together into a structured, practical workflow—one that mimics the process you would follow in a real-world scenario, whether for a research project, a business application, or an experimental endeavor. This chapter provides a comprehensive guide for the implementation of quantum machine learning, guiding you through the crucial steps of problem definition, data preparation, approach selection, and result interpretation. Although it might be repetitive, this chapter intentionally wraps up previous code snippets to put in a more project-sense approach.

The goal here is to transition from theory to practice, offering a condensed yet structured sequence that integrates many of the techniques we have covered. Instead of discussing each method in isolation, we'll now arrange them in a logical order, allowing you to see how they can be applied step by step. By following this chapter, you will gain insight into how to approach a real-world machine learning task, choose the appropriate quantum or classical models, and evaluate their performance effectively.

To ensure a well-rounded and comparative approach, we'll work with two distinct datasets, each representing a different industry: finance and healthcare. The classification problems in these datasets will allow us to evaluate the effectiveness of a quantum-based technique in two different domains and critically compare them against classical machine learning methods. This will help us determine where quantum models provide an advantage and where classical alternatives remain competitive.

We begin by finding the right problem to solve, an essential step in determining whether a quantum approach is necessary or beneficial. Next, we examine the dataset, considering its complexity and size—two factors that significantly impact the feasibility of using quantum techniques.

Once the data is prepared, we move to one of the most critical phases: finding the most suitable alternative. In this case we'll use Chapter's 7 approach of MKL and Chapter's 8 of VQC and autoencoders.

Finally, we focus on interpreting the outcome and discussing potential caveats. Analyzing the results requires understanding not just accuracy or AUC scores but also how quantum methods scale, their reliability, and whether they provide meaningful improvements over classical baselines. We'll highlight practical concerns such as use of simulators, hardware limitations, optimization challenges, and hybrid implementations, helping you make informed decisions when deploying quantum models in real-world scenarios.

By the end of this chapter, you will have a complete, step-by-step framework for implementing quantum machine learning on real datasets.

Find the right problem to solve

While quantum machine learning extends beyond classification problems, classification remains one of the most widely applicable tasks across industries. The ability to categorize data into distinct labels—whether it's fraud versus non-fraud, default versus non-default, or healthy versus at-risk—makes classification a cornerstone of machine learning adoption in finance, healthcare, retail, manufacturing, and beyond. In finance, institutions continuously assess creditworthiness, predict loan defaults, and detect fraudulent transactions. Healthcare professionals use predictive models to diagnose conditions such as diabetes, heart disease, or even the likelihood of a stroke based on patient data. In retail, companies strive to predict customer behavior, determining who is likely to buy a product or engage with a marketing campaign. Manufacturing and supply chain management rely on predictive analytics to anticipate machinery failures, optimize logistics, and reduce downtime. Similarly, industries like energy, telecommunications, education, entertainment, legal compliance, and many more can benefit from machine learning solutions—and, if proven advantageous, quantum machine learning could push these solutions further.

In this chapter, we focus on two critical industries: healthcare and finance. These fields present unique challenges in terms of data size, complexity, and the impact of predictive accuracy. The selected datasets not only represent different scales—one being relatively small and the other larger—but also exhibit characteristics that make classification non-trivial, such as non-linear separability and potential redundancy in features. By testing quantum-based classification methods on these datasets, we aim to evaluate whether quantum approaches offer measurable advantages over classical machine learning. The key question is not whether quantum computing can solve classification problems—classical models already do this effectively—but whether quantum methods can provide better performance, greater efficiency, or new insights that classical approaches struggle to achieve.

Dataset: complexity and size

To bridge the gap between theory and practice, we'll work with two real-world datasets from the UCI Machine Learning Repository, a widely used collection of datasets for benchmarking machine learning models—Kaggle is another source of real-life datasets to experiment with. These datasets represent two distinct domains—healthcare and finance, providing a diverse testbed for quantum machine learning techniques. They also vary significantly in size and complexity, allowing us to explore how different quantum approaches scale across datasets with different characteristics. By comparing results against classical machine learning methods, we'll gain valuable insights into the practical performance of quantum techniques in real-world scenarios.

In the case of healthcare, we'll use the Pima Indians Diabetes Database, which is a well-known dataset in the medical field, used to predict whether a patient is likely to develop diabetes based on physiological measurements and personal health indicators. It contains 768 samples and 9 numerical features, each representing clinically relevant patient characteristics. The dataset was originally collected by the National Institute of Diabetes and Digestive and Kidney Diseases and has been widely studied in machine learning research. The target variable is binary (0 or 1), indicating whether a patient meets the diagnostic criteria for diabetes.

The dataset's features include:

- Number of pregnancies: The number of times the patient has been pregnant.
- Plasma glucose concentration: A measurement from an oral glucose tolerance test.
- Diastolic blood pressure: Blood pressure in mm Hg.
- Triceps skin fold thickness: A measure of body fat.
- 2-hour serum insulin: Insulin levels after a glucose load.
- Body mass index (BMI): Weight-to-height ratio used to assess obesity.
- Diabetes pedigree function: A metric indicating genetic susceptibility to diabetes.
- Age: The age of the patient.
- Class variable (0 or 1): The target label indicating the presence or absence of diabetes.

This dataset presents an interesting challenge for machine learning models due to the class imbalance—there are fewer positive cases of diabetes (people having diabetes) than negative ones. We'll explore whether quantum machine learning techniques can improve predictive performance over classical methods.

The second dataset related to finance focuses on credit card default prediction, a critical problem in the financial industry where institutions assess the likelihood of a customer defaulting on their credit card payments. This dataset is significantly larger than the diabetes dataset, containing 30,000 samples and 25 features. The larger size and increased complexity make it a suitable test case for evaluating the scalability of quantum methods.

The dataset includes features related to a customer's credit history, payment behavior, and outstanding balances. Some of the key features are:

- PAY_0 to PAY_6: Payment status for the last six months (values range from -1 for on-time payments to 9 for severe delinquency).
- BILL_AMT1 to BILL_AMT6: Bill statement amounts for the last six months.
- PAY_AMT1 to PAY_AMT6: Payment amounts made in the last six months.
- Age and other demographic information: While not included in this version, other versions of this dataset sometimes contain information such as gender, education, and marital status.

The goal is to predict whether a customer will default on their credit card payment (not being able to pay) in the following month, which is represented by a binary target variable (0 for no default, 1 for default). This problem is particularly challenging due to the complex financial behaviors involved, as well as the need for models that can capture non-linear relationships within high-dimensional data. To avoid any confusion, note that, the convention used in such classification problems, as presented in both examples, is that the *default class* is the class that we are interested in detecting—patient having diabetes, not being able to pay, etc—and is referred to as the positive class (class 1), whereas the negative class is the normal or standard state without the condition (class 0).

When analyzing the complexity of these datasets, we need to consider several factors, including the number of features, correlations between variables, class distribution, and estimated intrinsic dimensionality. These factors help us understand how difficult it might be for a machine learning model—whether classical or quantum—to find meaningful patterns. Intrinsic dimensionality is particularly important because it tells us the true number of independent factors driving the variability in the data, which might be much lower than the raw number of features. If the intrinsic dimensionality is significantly smaller than the total number of recorded variables, it suggests that the dataset contains redundancy and that many features are not providing unique information.

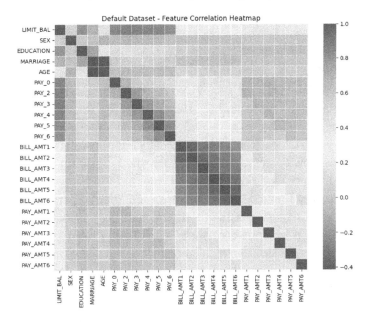

Figure 25

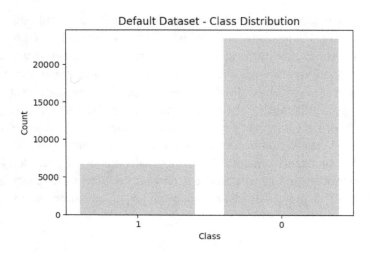

Figure 26

The Default Dataset, related to credit card defaults, presents a challenge due to its high-dimensional feature space. The correlation heatmap reveals strong relationships among some variables (red values indicate high correlation, blue values low correlation), particularly the repayment statuses across different months and bill amounts. This suggests that a few key financial behaviors are predictive of default risk, but redundancy exists within the dataset, meaning some features might not contribute significantly beyond others. The class distribution highlights an inherent imbalance, with a significantly higher number of non-default cases than default cases. This imbalance complicates training because models may develop a bias toward predicting the majority class unless corrective measures like resampling or cost-sensitive learning are used. Additionally, the estimated intrinsic dimensionality of the dataset is around 10.27, indicating that despite having 25 features, the true number of independent factors influencing the outcome is lower. This suggests that dimensionality reduction techniques like PCA or LDA could help in simplifying the feature space without losing essential information.

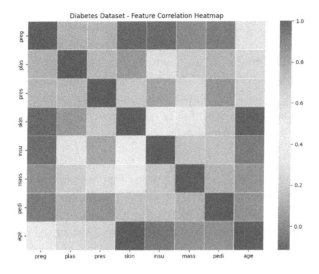

Figure 27

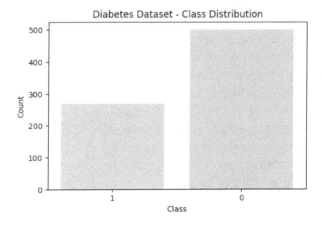

Figure 28

The Diabetes Dataset, which aims to predict diabetes onset, is considerably smaller. This dataset's correlation heatmap shows weaker relationships among variables, meaning that each feature might contribute more uniquely to the prediction task. The class distribution is less imbalanced compared to the credit default dataset, but still shows a higher proportion of non-diabetic cases, which may impact classification performance. With an intrinsic dimensionality of 6.62, this dataset is more compact, suggesting that while feature selection and dimensionality reduction could still be useful, they are not as crucial as in the higher-dimensional default dataset.

The t-SNE and PCA visualizations further reinforce this by showing that the separation between classes is not always clear in both datasets, indicating that simple linear models may struggle to capture the underlying structure of the data. This suggests that non-linear decision boundaries, such as those introduced by kernel methods or quantum-enhanced models, might be necessary to map the data into a space where separation becomes more distinct. Rather than contradicting the use of kernels, these observations highlight their importance—kernel-based methods are specifically designed to transform data into higher-dimensional representations where complex patterns become more discernible. Given the estimated intrinsic dimensionalities of both datasets, leveraging non-linear mappings through kernel techniques or quantum feature maps could provide a more effective approach to classification, ensuring that intricate relationships between features are captured and utilized for better predictive accuracy.

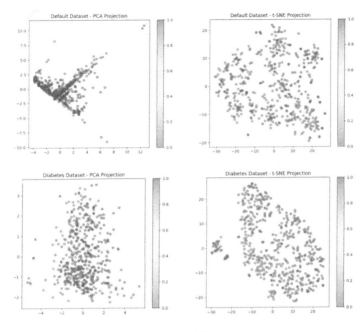

Figure 29

In summary, the Default Dataset poses challenges due to its high dimensionality, redundancy among variables, and strong class imbalance, making it well-suited for techniques that can handle these complexities, such as kernel methods or quantum-enhanced models. The Diabetes Dataset, while smaller and less complex, still requires careful handling of feature interactions and non-linearity to make effective predictions. Both datasets serve as useful benchmarks for comparing classical and quantum machine learning techniques, allowing us to explore how quantum models deal with different levels of complexity and data structures.

Data preprocessing

Before diving into modeling, we need to prepare our dataset to ensure it's clean, structured, and optimized for learning. The preprocessing phase is crucial because the quality of input data directly affects the performance of both classical and quantum machine learning models. Here, we'll go through the key steps: loading the data, handling missing values, removing redundant features, clustering variables, reducing dimensionality, and normalizing the dataset.

We start by loading the dataset and ensuring all its values are numerical. Since missing values can introduce biases or errors, we handle them by filling them with zero. This is a simple imputation method, but depending on the problem, other techniques like mean imputation or regression-based estimations could be considered.

```python
import numpy as np
import pandas as pd

# Load the dataset for diabetes

df = pd.read_csv("diabetes_dataset.csv")
df = df.astype(float).fillna(0)

# Load the dataset for default

df = pd.read_csv("default_dataset.csv")
df = df.astype(float).fillna(0)
```

Once we have our dataset structured, we need to split it into training and testing sets. The training set is used for model learning, while the test set helps evaluate its performance on unseen data. We allocate 80% of the dataset to training and the remaining 20% to testing.

```
from sklearn.model_selection import train_test_split

# Split dataset into training and test sets for diabetes

X_train, X_test, y_train, y_test = train_test_split(
        df.drop(["class"], axis=1),
        df["class"],
        test_size=0.2,
        random_state=42
)

# Split dataset into training and test sets for default

X_train, X_test, y_train, y_test = train_test_split(
        df.drop(['default.payment.next.month', 'ID'],
axis="columns"),
        df['default.payment.next.month'],
        test_size=0.2,
        random_state=42
)
```

Many datasets contain features that are constant across all samples, meaning they don't contribute any useful information to the classification process. These features add unnecessary complexity and computational cost without improving the model's performance. We remove them to ensure our dataset is streamlined.

```
# Drop constant columns

constant_columns = X_train.columns[X_train.nunique() == 1]
X_train = X_train.drop(columns=constant_columns)
X_test = X_test.drop(columns=constant_columns)
```

A crucial step in preprocessing is understanding how different features relate to the target variable. By computing feature correlations, we can use the metric to group the features later and then apply LDA. When applying LDA for binary classification, the transformation process results in only one reduced-dimension feature because LDA is designed to maximize class separability by projecting data onto a single axis. This is a fundamental limitation in the binary case, as LDA finds only one direction that best separates the two classes, leading to the loss of multiple independent feature dimensions that could hold valuable information.

To retain more than just one transformed feature, clustering is a good option. By grouping features into clusters based on similarity or correlation, we can apply LDA separately to each cluster, ensuring that each subset of features gets its own discriminative projection rather than forcing the entire dataset onto a single axis. This approach preserves more structural information, as different clusters may capture distinct patterns relevant to the classification task.

```
from sklearn.cluster import KMeans
import numpy as np



# Calculate correlations for clustering

correlations = X_train.corrwith(y_train)
correlations_reshaped = np.reshape(correlations.values, (-1, 1))
```

Now, instead of manually selecting important features, we use K-Means clustering to group similar features based on their correlation with the target variable. By organizing features into clusters, we can extract meaningful representations while reducing redundancy. Here with n_clusters you will determine how many features you will end up with and also subsequent qubits to be used.

```
# Clustering features into groups

kmeans =
KMeans(n_clusters=2,random_state=0).fit(correlations_reshaped)
clusters = kmeans.labels_
groups = [np.where(clusters == i)[0] for i in range(2)]
```

After clustering, we apply LDA to extract key features that best separate the classes.

```
from sklearn.discriminant_analysis import
LinearDiscriminantAnalysis as LDA

# Apply LDA for dimensionality reduction

features_lda = np.empty((X_train.shape[0], 2))
features_lda_test = np.empty((X_test.shape[0], 2))

for i, group in enumerate(groups):
        lda = LDA(n_components=1)
        features_lda[:, i] =
lda.fit_transform(X_train.iloc[:, group], y_train).ravel()
        features_lda_test[:, i] =
lda.transform(X_test.iloc[:, group]).ravel()
```

Since the transformed features may have different numerical scales, we apply standardization to ensure that all attributes contribute equally to the learning process.

```
from sklearn.preprocessing import StandardScaler

# Normalize features for QSVC

scaler_qsvc = StandardScaler().fit(features_lda)
X_train_qsvc = scaler_qsvc.transform(features_lda)
X_test_qsvc = scaler_qsvc.transform(features_lda_test)
```

Quantum models usually operate with qubits representing each feature, therefore, we determine the number of qubits required based on our reduced dataset. Here, n_qubits is set to match the transformed feature space from LDA.

```
# Update the number of qubits based on LDA output

n_qubits = X_train_qsvc.shape[1]
```

Applying quantum techniques

To avoid repeating the code snippets, you can follow the GitHub repository code for the two datasets or cases, or jump to Chapter's 7 and 8 to review the code of VQC with autoencoders and MKL. The first one will be used for the Default Dataset and the second for Diabetes Dataset.

In the finance case of predicting default, we need to reduce the sample size from near 30,000 to 5,000 to avoid computational complexity and not take several hours to run locally.

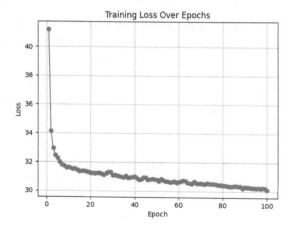

Figure 30

It's easy to see how epochs with a mix of reconstruction loss and classification loss were able to evolve and give us our first results by using an autoencoder for the encoding part and a variational classification for the classification part. Here is an example of what you would see printed in the epochs evolution:

```
Epoch 1/100, Total Loss: 41.1826, Reconstruction Loss: 3.0775,
Classification Loss: 79.2876
Epoch 2/100, Total Loss: 34.1196, Reconstruction Loss: 2.0317,
Classification Loss: 66.2075
Epoch 3/100, Total Loss: 32.9590, Reconstruction Loss: 1.2029,
Classification Loss: 64.7151
```

Once the model finishes the training phase, you can evaluate the outcome.

```
Test Accuracy: 0.8180
Test AUC: 0.7521
Test KS Statistic: 0.4029
```

For the Diabetes Dataset we'll use the MKL alignment perspective. After running, you should see this final outcome.

```
-----------------------------------------------------------

                          Summary

-----------------------------------------------------------

(CVXPY) Feb 21 12:08:20 PM: Problem status: optimal
(CVXPY) Feb 21 12:08:20 PM: Optimal value: 2.342e+04
(CVXPY) Feb 21 12:08:20 PM: Compilation took 8.740e-01 seconds
(CVXPY) Feb 21 12:08:20 PM: Solver (including time spent in
interface) took 1.032e-03 seconds

Test Accuracy: 0.7143
Test AUC: 0.8244
Test KS Statistic: 0.5010
```

And also including the heatmap of the combined Kernel.

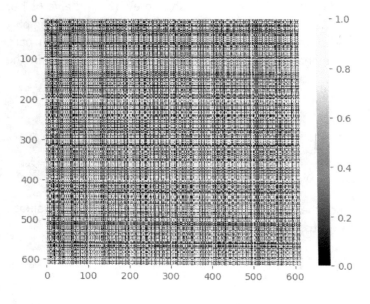

Figure 31

Benchmark

Now that we have explored how a quantum technique might be useful let's work on the comparison with classical methods. To conduct this benchmark, we'll use three classical models that are widely used in machine learning:

1. Support Vector Machine (SVM) – A purely classical approach of what we used several times in the book.
2. Logistic Regression (LR) – A simple yet effective model for binary classification, often used as a baseline in machine learning.

3. XGBoost (XGB) – A gradient boosting framework known for its high performance in structured data classification.

Each of these models will be trained and tested on the same dataset used in the previous execution, ensuring a fair comparison between quantum and classical approaches.

The first step is to load the dataset and perform a more basic preprocessing.

```python
import pandas as pd
import numpy as np
from sklearn.model_selection import train_test_split
from sklearn.preprocessing import StandardScaler




# Load the dataset for diabetes

df = pd.read_csv("diabetes_dataset.csv")
df = df.astype(float).fillna(0)

# Load the dataset for default

df = pd.read_csv("default_dataset.csv")
df = df.astype(float).fillna(0)

# Split dataset into training and test sets for diabetes

X_train, X_test, y_train, y_test = train_test_split(
        df.drop(["class"], axis=1),
        df["class"],
        test_size=0.2,
        random_state=42
)

# Split dataset into training and test sets for default

X_train, X_test, y_train, y_test = train_test_split(
        df.drop(['default.payment.next.month', 'ID'],
```

```
axis="columns"),
        df['default.payment.next.month'],
        test_size=0.2,
        random_state=42
)
```

This ensures that both the training and testing sets maintain the original class distribution, reducing the risk of bias in model evaluation. Also we use the exact same setup of the MKL.

Since machine learning models perform best when input features are normalized, we apply standardization. This scales the features to have zero mean and unit variance, ensuring that models like SVM and Logistic Regression are not negatively affected by differences in feature scales.

```
# Standardize the features

scaler = StandardScaler()
X_train = scaler.fit_transform(X_train)
X_test = scaler.transform(X_test)
```

We now initialize the three machine learning models. Each model has been carefully chosen for its strengths:

- SVM: Uses a non-linear decision boundary that is particularly effective when data is not linearly separable.
- Logistic Regression: A simple, interpretable model that serves as a strong baseline.
- XGBoost: A gradient boosting model that handles feature importance and non-linearity efficiently.

```
from sklearn.svm import SVC
from sklearn.linear_model import LogisticRegression
from xgboost import XGBClassifier


# Initialize models

svm_model = SVC(probability=True, random_state=42)
lr_model = LogisticRegression(random_state=42,
max_iter=200000)  # Increased max_iter to ensure convergence
xgb_model = XGBClassifier(eval_metric="logloss",
random_state=42, max_depth=3, n_estimators=50)
```

Each model is configured with parameters that optimize its performance, such as setting `max_iter` to prevent premature stopping in logistic regression and choosing `max_depth=3` in XGBoost to balance model complexity and generalization.

Once the models are initialized, we train them on the preprocessed dataset.

```
# Train models

svm_model.fit(X_train, y_train)
lr_model.fit(X_train, y_train)
xgb_model.fit(X_train, y_train)
```

At this stage, each model learns patterns from the training data, adjusting its internal parameters to best separate the classes

After training, the models need to be evaluated on unseen test data. Instead of only predicting binary class labels (0 or 1), we extract probability scores per class for each instance. This allows us to use AUC (Area Under the Curve) and KS Statistic as evaluation metrics.

```
# Make predictions

svm_probs = svm_model.predict_proba(X_test)[:, 1]
lr_probs = lr_model.predict_proba(X_test)[:, 1]
xgb_probs = xgb_model.predict_proba(X_test)[:, 1]
```

Each model outputs a probability score, which helps assess how confident the model is about its predictions.

To complement the AUC score, we use the Kolmogorov-Smirnov (KS) statistic, which measures how well-separated the predicted scores of positive and negative classes are.

```
def ks_stat(y_true, probs):
        df = pd.DataFrame({"y_true": y_true, "probs": probs})
        df = df.sort_values("probs")
        df["cum_event"] = (df["y_true"] == 1).cumsum()
        df["cum_non_event"] = (df["y_true"] == 0).cumsum()
        total_event = df["cum_event"].iloc[-1]
        total_non_event = df["cum_non_event"].iloc[-1]
        df["event_rate"] = df["cum_event"] / total_event
        df["non_event_rate"] = df["cum_non_event"] /
total_non_event
        ks = (df["event_rate"] -
df["non_event_rate"]).abs().max()
        return ks




# Calculate KS statistics

svm_ks = ks_stat(y_test, svm_probs)
lr_ks = ks_stat(y_test, lr_probs)
xgb_ks = ks_stat(y_test, xgb_probs)
```

A higher KS statistic indicates better model separation between classes, which is crucial to understand the quality of the model.

To benchmark the performance, we compute Accuracy, AUC, KS Statistic, and a Classification Report for each model.

```
from sklearn.metrics import accuracy_score,
classification_report, roc_auc_score


# Evaluate models

results = {
        "SVM": {
                "Accuracy": accuracy_score(y_test,
svm_model.predict(X_test)),
                "AUC": roc_auc_score(y_test, svm_probs),
                "KS": svm_ks
        },
        "Logistic Regression": {
                "Accuracy": accuracy_score(y_test,
lr_model.predict(X_test)),
                "AUC": roc_auc_score(y_test, lr_probs),
                "KS": lr_ks
        },
        "XGBoost": {
                "Accuracy": accuracy_score(y_test,
xgb_model.predict(X_test)),
                "AUC": roc_auc_score(y_test, xgb_probs),
                "KS": xgb_ks
        }
}
```

This stores all evaluation metrics for easy comparison.

Finally, we print the results in a structured format for comparison.

```
# Print the results

for model, metrics in results.items():
        print(f"=== {model} ===")
        print(f"Accuracy: {metrics['Accuracy']:.4f}")
        print(f"AUC: {metrics['AUC']:.4f}")
        print(f"KS Statistic: {metrics['KS']:.4f}")
        print("\n")
```

This step summarizes how each classical model performs on the dataset.

Here, we have the results of the Default Dataset using the same sample size we used for the quantum approach:

```
=== SVM ===

Accuracy: 0.808
AUC: 0.6976
KS Statistic: 0.3384

=== Logistic Regression ===

Accuracy: 0.8030
AUC: 0.7117
KS Statistic: 0.3549

=== XGBoost ===

Accuracy: 0.8090
AUC: 0.7458
KS Statistic: 0.3668
```

And here, the results on the Diabetes Dataset:

```
=== SVM ===

Accuracy: 0.7532
AUC: 0.7924
KS Statistic: 0.4833

=== Logistic Regression ===

Accuracy: 0.7143
AUC: 0.8230
KS Statistic: 0.5419

=== XGBoost ===

Accuracy: 0.7597
AUC: 0.8213
KS Statistic: 0.5519
```

Interpreting the outcome

The results of our benchmarking between quantum and classical models reveal crucial insights into how different approaches handle complex classification tasks. While quantum models demonstrate compelling advantages in some cases, they do not consistently outperform classical techniques across all datasets, indicating that their effectiveness is highly dependent on data characteristics and problem structure.

In the Default Dataset, the VQC combined with an autoencoder outperformed all classical models in accuracy, AUC, and KS statistics. This suggests that the quantum-enhanced feature extraction provided a more effective transformation of the data, capturing subtle relationships that classical models struggled to learn efficiently. The higher KS statistic is particularly relevant, as it indicates a greater ability to separate defaulting from non-defaulting clients, a key requirement in financial risk modeling. However, the difference between the quantum model and XGBoost was relatively small, raising the question of whether the computational cost of running quantum-enhanced models is justified when an optimized classical approach delivers similar results.

In contrast, the Diabetes Dataset presented a different outcome. The Multiple Kernel Learning (MKL) approach using quantum kernels achieved a competitive AUC but was outperformed by logistic regression and XGBoost in accuracy and KS statistics. This result challenges the assumption that quantum kernels always provide superior feature representations. Given the relatively low intrinsic dimensionality of this dataset, classical models were likely able to capture most of the predictive variance without requiring the complex transformations that quantum kernels introduce. Additionally, while quantum kernel alignment optimized the combination of multiple feature mappings, it did not create a significant enough separation in the feature space to outperform classical approaches fully.

The key takeaway from these results is that quantum machine learning can be beneficial, but its impact depends on the dataset's complexity and structure. The credit card default dataset, with its high intrinsic dimensionality and strong feature correlations, benefited from quantum-enhanced transformations that created more effective decision boundaries. In contrast, the Diabetes Dataset, with lower dimensionality and more independently informative features, saw little benefit from quantum techniques, as classical methods were already well-suited to the task.

The performance of XGBoost in both datasets further underscores that well-optimized classical models remain powerful contenders. This algorithm consistently delivered results close to, and sometimes better than, the quantum models, showing that advanced ensemble learning techniques can still handle complex decision boundaries effectively. This finding suggests that quantum models must demonstrate a clear and consistent advantage over classical techniques to justify their use, particularly when computational resources and scalability are considerations.

Another notable observation is that quantum models improved decision boundaries, as seen in the higher KS statistics for the Default Dataset. The ability of quantum models to create more effective separations between classes is particularly valuable in domains where misclassification can have significant consequences, such as fraud detection, credit risk assessment, and medical diagnosis. This suggests that while quantum models may not always lead to higher overall accuracy, they can provide better insights into class separability, potentially improving interpretability and robustness in high-stakes applications.

These results highlight the importance of carefully selecting when and where to apply quantum models. While they hold promise, especially for datasets with high intrinsic dimensionality and nonlinear interactions, they are not a universal solution that automatically outperforms classical approaches. A more practical strategy would be to integrate quantum models selectively, using them for feature extraction or kernel learning while relying on classical machine learning for final decision-making. This hybrid approach ensures that quantum techniques are applied where they provide the most benefit while leveraging the efficiency of classical models where they still excel.

Disappointed? You shouldn't be. Like classical models, the quantum machine learning techniques have different approaches, parameters, and tweaks that you can do to keep evaluating if different architectures are better than others for your dataset. This book is pursuing a realistic state of the art of QML and not trying to engage you with toy models having a 1.0 accuracy or AUC outcome. In the next section, we'll address all of those different angles that you should consider or keep in mind.

Caveats

Throughout this journey, we have explored a diverse range of quantum machine learning techniques, benchmarked them against classical methods, and examined their performance in practical scenarios. While the potential of QML is undeniable, it's equally important to acknowledge the challenges that remain and the caveats that must be considered before jumping to conclusions about quantum advantage. The field is still in its infancy, and as exciting as these advancements are, responsible experimentation, rigorous evaluation, and realistic expectations are crucial for meaningful progress.

One of the most pressing concerns in QML research is the reliance on toy datasets such as MNIST and Iris. While these datasets are valuable for initial testing and proof-of-concept demonstrations, they do not reflect the complexity of real-world problems. Too often, research claims impressive quantum results on these simplified datasets, only to fail when applied to actual industry challenges. The need for more realistic benchmarks is evident—datasets with high-dimensional, noisy, and heterogeneous features, such as those in finance, healthcare, and cybersecurity, will serve as better testbeds for assessing whether quantum models can truly outperform classical alternatives.

Another limitation frequently overlooked in QML research is the improper comparison of models. Comparing QSVMs directly to classical SVMs, for example, is misleading because quantum kernels inherently transform feature spaces differently. Instead, quantum models should be benchmarked against state-of-the-art classical techniques like gradient boosting, deep learning, or ensemble models, which are the true competitors in practical applications. This ensures that claims of quantum advantage are not based on artificial baselines but on genuine advancements over the best available classical methods. Similarly, researchers must move beyond accuracy as the sole performance metric. In fields like fraud detection, financial risk assessment, and medical diagnosis, datasets are often imbalanced, meaning that accuracy alone can be highly misleading. More informative metrics, such as AUC, KS statistic, MCC, and F1-score, provide a clearer picture of a model's effectiveness. A superficial claim of 99% accuracy means little if the dataset is 99% one class and the model is simply predicting the majority class every time.

Beyond benchmarking, there are deeper theoretical and practical challenges in QML that still require solutions. One major hurdle is scalability. As we increase the number of qubits, quantum models face issues like barren plateaus—regions in the optimization landscape where gradients vanish, making training nearly impossible. Finding ways to avoid these pitfalls, whether through improved initialization techniques, hybrid classical-quantum training strategies, or structured ansätze, is essential for making QML truly practical. Likewise, data encoding remains a bottleneck; encoding classical data into quantum states efficiently is still a challenge, and poorly designed feature maps can limit a quantum model's expressivity. Research on adaptive encoding methods that dynamically select the best representation for a given dataset is crucial.

Furthermore, it's essential to acknowledge that today's quantum hardware is still in the NISQ era, meaning that errors and decoherence significantly impact performance. Without effective error mitigation techniques, real-world deployment remains difficult. While quantum simulators provide a glimpse into potential advantages, true breakthroughs will require hardware improvements that allow quantum circuits to run with less noise and greater depth. This is why efforts should focus not just on abstract algorithmic improvements but on practical implementations that leverage the constraints of existing quantum devices.

Despite these challenges, there are promising avenues where QML might have a meaningful impact. One particularly exciting direction is the potential for hybrid models, where quantum methods are integrated with classical approaches rather than replacing them entirely (that probably will never happen). Instead of expecting QML to outperform every classical method, we should investigate how quantum models can enhance certain aspects of machine learning pipelines, such as feature selection, kernel learning, or solving combinatorial optimization subproblems more efficiently. Combining quantum circuits with deep learning architectures, leveraging quantum kernels alongside traditional methods, or using quantum-enhanced heuristics within broader ML workflows could be the key to unlocking quantum's practical benefits.

Ultimately, responsible progress in QML means acknowledging its current limitations while continuing to push forward with rigorous, meaningful research. The field does not need exaggerated claims of superiority over classical models but rather well-founded studies that explore when and where quantum methods provide real, measurable improvements. As quantum hardware matures and theoretical insights evolve, the potential for breakthrough applications will become clearer—but only if we stay grounded in scientific rigor, practical benchmarks, and a willingness to challenge our assumptions.

So as we close this chapter, the takeaway is not that quantum machine learning is an immediate replacement for classical approaches, but that it represents a new frontier with unique opportunities and open challenges. Whether you are a researcher, practitioner, or business leader exploring these ideas, the goal should be to experiment thoughtfully, compare fairly, and seek out the problems where quantum models can truly add value. The road ahead is filled with both obstacles and potential, but with careful exploration, we may find that QML is not just a passing trend but a fundamental shift in the way we approach machine learning and optimization.

Further Reading

Deep Learning in Finance: A Survey of Applications and Techniques:
https://www.mdpi.com/2673-2688/5/4/101

A Comprehensive Review on Machine Learning in Healthcare Industry: Classification, Restrictions, Opportunities and Challenges:
https://pmc.ncbi.nlm.nih.gov/articles/PMC10180678/

AI in retail:
https://www.ibm.com/think/topics/ai-in-retail

Role of Machine Learning in Manufacturing Sector:
https://www.researchgate.net/publication/364091962_Role_of_Machine_Learning_in_Manufacturing_Sector

Machine learning for a sustainable energy future:
https://www.nature.com/articles/s41578-022-00490-5

Machine learning use cases: how to design ML architectures for today's telecom systems:
https://www.ericsson.com/en/blog/2021/5/machine-learning-use-cases-in-telecom

A Brief Review of Quantum Machine Learning for Financial Services:
https://arxiv.org/abs/2407.12618

Quantum Machine Learning Revolution in Healthcare: A Systematic Review of Emerging Perspectives and Applications: https://ieeexplore.ieee.org/document/10398184

The UC Irvine Machine Learning Repository: https://archive.ics.uci.edu/

Default of credit card clients, Kaggle dataset: https://www.kaggle.com/datasets/mariosfish/default-of-credit-card-clients

Pima Indians Diabetes Database, Kaggle dataset: https://www.kaggle.com/datasets/uciml/pima-indians-diabetes-database

Data preprocessing impact on machine learning algorithm performance: https://www.degruyter.com/document/doi/10.1515/comp-2022-0278/html

XGBoost: https://www.nvidia.com/en-eu/glossary/xgboost/

Computing the Two-Sided Kolmogorov-Smirnov Distribution: https://www.jstatsoft.org/article/view/v039i11

Chapter Figures

We generated Figures 25-31 from the code snippets discussed here, and the full codes are in Jupyter notebooks in the book's GitHub repository Chapter 10.